## WHEN IN THE COURSE OF HUMAN EVENTS . . .

The others my age are all talking "retire"
While I'm just getting a start.
My friends are ready to hang it all up
And I'm just shifting from "park."
My family's all shouting, "Go after it, Mom!"
My mother says, "Why should you go?"
Back off a bit, folks — let me find my own way!
It's years since I've wanted to grow!

I'm lucky as hell just to see the brass ring,
To find a direction — a role —
A way to play catch-up now my other work's done
And I'm free to consider a goal.
A room of my own, as Virginia Woolf said,
Where I can be think
While my whole world looks on a
I just hope to God they'l

❦

# THERE'S MORE TO ME
# THAN I'VE USED YET

FRANCES WEAVER

*With incidental drawings
from the author's sketchbook*

*Cover by Roger Roth*

**MIDLIFE MUSINGS**

Saratoga Springs
New York
1994

ISBN 0-9617930-6-6

Cover design:
Melanie Wegner
Bear Canyon Creative
Albuquerque, New Mexico

Book design, editing and production:
Wallace W. Abbey
Piñon Consulting
Pueblo, Colorado

Much of the contents of this book has appeared previously in the
Pueblo (Colorado) *Chieftain*, in the Saratoga Springs (New York)
*Saratogian*, or in earlier books by Frances Weaver

Printed in the United States of America

10 9 8 7 6 5 4 3 2 1

Published by
Midlife Musings
P. O. Box 970
Saratoga Springs, New York 12866

FOR . . .

those understanding readers, tolerant viewers, agreeable
editors, patient publishers, encouraging mentors, and my
supportive family — the enablers of this wondrous part of
my life — I offer gratitude. But it is rightfully to my
husband, who devoted the best years of his life to teaching
me humility and how to drive, that this book is dedicated.
Without all these people, none of my adventures of
advanced age would have happened.

☙

# CONTENTS

Introduction                                    IX

I.      Dear John                               2

II.     Aging? What's That?                     7

III.    I've Been Thinking . . .                23

IV.     On Traveling                            47

V.      My Special Worlds                       75

VI.     Take It from Me!                        93

VII.    Weavers, Allisons, and Company          123

VIII.   Vesta                                   144

# INTRODUCTION

Shelves and racks of CDs and other recordings in discount stores across the nation offer collections of the works of everyone from Beethoven to Bob Newhart to Garth Brooks. Should Mozart return to this earth he might be enchanted by our selections of his "greatest hits." Then again, the choices might not please him at all.

Unlike Mozart and his masterpieces, two hundred years from now not one soul will care about or know about "Frances Weaver's Greatest Hits," but at the close of my tenth year as a columnist I feel compelled to put together the columns I have enjoyed most during this unexpected, un-planned-for turn of events in my life.

For a recycled housewife, the very existence of nearly five hundred weekly columns about subjects ranging from kiteflying to Turkish cuisine can be regarded as an astonishment. My contention that older women can (and should!) create interest and purpose in their own lives after the children have grown and the house is quiet has led me to expanded horizons I never imagined in my wildest dreams. One step at a time.

With each step I have learned. Some of the lessons were painful, like going all the way to Spokane to address a huge crowd of seniors who never showed up — not one! Others have been almost transcendent, like the young woman in Seattle who exclaimed, "You saved my mother's life," referring to my recommendations for accepting widowhood as an expectable part of our lives. Learning to trust ourselves.

Some of my lessons have been academic. Life as a fifty-nine-year-old college freshman gave me a fresh start, a new view of myself. Since then.

Smithsonian tours and seminars, writers' conferences, and Elderhostel have jogged my brain and enlivened my curiosity.

All of that has happened in response to my commitment to writing regularly and the consequent opportunity to "spread my own word" by public television. In this book you will encounter old friends and new experiences, just as I have found them. You will also find a joy of living that encompasses an appreciation for the good years past and the bright world yet to come.

Enjoy!

*Frances Weaver*
Pueblo, Colorado
January, 1994

❧

## I. DEAR JOHN

How do men envision their wives as widows? As whiners? Helpless? Capable? Resourceful? Foolish? Competent? Or do men generally contemplate such matters at all?

How often does any man or woman speculate upon how he or she would manage life as the surviving spouse? Not only money management here. We're talking life.

What influence does any married man have on the way his wife accepts widowhood? Should married men — can husbands — help their wives face the probability of widowhood, addressing more than financial planning and considering the quality of life typical of most widows?

Or do most men just consider 'til-death-do-us-part good enough and assume she'll turn out like her mother?

Those questions crop up more and more frequently in my conversations with people my age and older. I'm sixty-eight. For more than thirteen years after the death of my husband I've worked at being a self-reliant single woman. (Twenty per cent of my entire life we're talking here, not an unusual figure.)

I find myself tempted to say, "my husband, the surgeon," since his career always ranked uppermost in our married and family life. With other couples, other relationships, the emphasis differs. The basic question remains the same: "What sort of a widow do you expect your wife to be? Is that her responsibility alone?"

I don't want to sound mean, but the way a woman copes with the reality of the death of her husband tells the world a great deal about both of those people. I listen to some whiners, who might even be termed Perennial Mourners, whose opening line of any conversation never varies. Recitals of loneliness, ailments, problems, always prefaced by, "You know, dear, it's been sixteen years since I lost Fred," have been known to send acquaintances more tolerant than me into severe depression. Especially around Christmas.

The temptation is to set her straight, not pulling any punches. In the first place, Fred is not lost. Mrs. Mournful knows exactly where he is. In the second place, Fred was probably a nice-enough man who would be embarrassed by this self-pitying complainer. But most of all, I cannot escape the feeling that if Fred had spent some time and attention during their forty years of wedded bliss giving that wife of his some idea of her own worth, her own value in this life, she wouldn't waste so much time bemoaning the fact that her husband is no longer at her side — realizing that all of the bemoaning in the world cannot bring him back.

That's what these essays (letters) are about. Looking ahead. We need not take a morbid or unseemly approach. We need only take a good hard look at the realities and logical expectations of life as it really is, and will be.

One last question: How would my own husband have envisioned me as a widow? Broke.

Frequently during these years as a single in my sixties I have wished I could write to John. Send him some snapshots, even. Often I'd like to say, "I told you so." Once in a while I'd like to say, "You didn't think I could handle this, did you?" Rarely am I tempted to say, "Hey, doctor, aren't you proud?" Most often, sometimes to my surprise, I just want to say, "Thanks."

Our courtship and engagement days were spent writing letters to each other. John Weaver served most of World War II in the Army getting his pre-med education and declaring his love via letters at least once every day to the girl he left in college back in Kansas. Now he has left that girl for good, but letters seem the most appropriate vehicle for the message of this moment: "We gave it our best shot, John, but I wish we had both understood . . ."

One letter at a time. Something like this:

Dear John,

The Bears are beating the Vikings. That same old Sunday-afternoon sound brings you right up front here. I am now sitting in the Atlanta airport, corner table in a crowded bar. I cannot even see the screen of the TV but the sound suffices. Sunday afternoon football. This provides an appropriate backdrop for commencing a series of letters to you even though you haven't watched or slept through the past thirteen NFL seasons.

I'll not see (hear) all of this game because I have a plane to catch. Next stop, LaGuardia; then Princeton, Detroit, Saratoga Springs, Rome (New York), and Portland, Oregon, before I get back to Pueblo in a couple of weeks. I'll explain all of this travel later. Right now I'm caught up in this football crowd.

Surely you haven't forgotten sleeping in front of TV, especially football. Remember the Monday night when I suggested, "Why don't you just go to bed if you're so tired?"

You said, "What time is it?"

I said, "Nine o'clock."

You said, "Too early for bed. Wake me at nine-thirty."

Men's voices, men's laughter, men's shop talk about cars, small talk about big deals — all this talk drifts over to the corner — but football sounds rule the day. Sunday sounds of you and me and the Broncos and the Raiders and the Redskins and the Rams. So I choose this place to reminisce, writing a letter to you as we approach our fourteenth anniversary: mine of being single, yours of being dead.

Saying "dead" stops most people in their tracks, you know, John. You used to complain about that a lot — the patients who could not bring themselves to facing the facts of living and dying, so they couldn't say "dead" right out loud. They used some euphemism like "passed away." You had a tendency to be pretty judgmental about that. How you would have loved a lady I met in Portland, Oregon, who claimed the oft-used statement, "I lost my husband," sounds careless, like "I can't find my eyeglasses." You did dislike my habit of saying "you know" all the time, too, John. Did you notice it in the first of this paragraph? Sorry.

In some ways, death might have separated us just yesterday. Other ways, it seems ages since we were at home in Beulah and you went up to bed before I did on that Thursday night. An hour later, you didn't reach to turn off the light over your side of the bed when I came up. Then I knew.

John, do you remember how we laughed and made fun of those endless Christmas letters and poems we used to get about the wonders of everyone else's families? Patty bragged about kids who blew horns and shot baskets while she "baked the best home-made bread on the block." Aunt Grace tried to tell us all about Evelyn's twenty-one living children and their families on the back of one Hallmark card. This letter will be a lot like that.

Rolling more than a decade into one series of letters could be a real bore. I'll skip some details, and put in a few laughs as we go along. Whenever the kids and I start reminiscing we always wind up laughing. I like to think that speaks well for our family. I also might strike a nerve or two to make you mad. Most of all, I want you to know how much a part of our lives you are now. The melody lingers on, as the girls back in Concordia used to say.

Incidentally, did I ever make it clear to you how sick I got of hearing about the girls in Concordia? Are all men that way about home-town sweethearts, or were those girls special?

Catching up on how much and how fast the world has changed in the past thirteen years would be a hopeless task. *Fax* and *Sprint* you can get along without knowing. I do harbor a vague feeling that you know a lot about what goes on around here. Your powers of observation always astounded me, particularly when I thought I'd gotten away with something. You saw. You knew. That has to be what made you such an extraordinary diagnostician. And I feel timid, like a little kid afraid of being scolded, as I write this now.

You managed to take a history and physical of everyone we met, patients or not. I picked up much of that from you and it comes in handy in this new part of my life. Thank you.

As a matter of strict fact, I can thank you for enhancing much of what my life has become since your sudden departure. Also, I find myself feeling cheated or at least short-changed by some of our married-life experiences. Looking at the grandkids, I regret the good times you've missed, but we cannot do much about that. That's what these letters are all about, John. After all these years I feel the need, the readiness, to go over it with you. Don't worry, I won't cause as much trauma as our monthly bouts with the checkbook. You might even enjoy this process. So relax, dear John, but keep your feet braced.

---

Dear John,

Do you wonder why I'm going to all this trouble, writing these letters? Well, at 11:11 p.m. on my sixty-sixth birthday, September 24, I can picture you out there somewhere in a flapping white robe, halo aglow, while I pick up this yellow tablet night after night, starting another paragraph or so to you.

Obviously, you and I shared a strong belief in some sort of afterlife even though we didn't talk about such things all that much. We had no need for such discussion, really. Your presence around here cannot be proven, only felt. I honestly don't expect you to commence breaking things around the house or showing up in mini-whirlwinds along the road. But you are here. Somehow.

I think a lot about our parents and their diametrically opposite concepts of living and dying and the importance of each to the other. Your mother never insisted that Joe be responsible for his own well-being and daily need. That equates with those husbands who shelter their wives from the details of keeping the checkbook or knowing about the insurance. One big difference: A woman who waits on her husband hand and foot is called "spineless" or stupid. A man who babies his wife and protects her from the reality of utility bills and monthly Visa payments is lovingly referred to as "devoted." Both of our sets of parents fit the mold in completely opposite ways. The newest buzzword for such couples is "co-dependent." I doubt you heard that much before 1980.

One point for our team, honey: Our system of paying bills, where I wrote the checks and you signed them, worked better than any I've heard of from other couples. Especially since we paid them out of *your* account. My allowance did household help and kids' spending money. I'm still not good at balancing the checking account, but at least I had a nodding acquaintance with the process. Come to think of it, you weren't too red hot at bank balances, either.

One explanation of the attitudes of so many people we know about "losing a spouse" can be found in a conversation I had with Benjy Brooks. You'd really like Benjy. She talks your language. Benjy is a pediatric surgeon down in DeBakey Land who is recognized all over the country for her work. First woman to do a lot of things. Now Benjy concentrates her attention and energies on ethics. Not just medical ethics; she quotes one of the dons at Cambridge, where she studied ethics for a year, as saying, "The trouble with you Americans is you consider death to be an option." That follows right along with your opinion that practitioners of medicine have oversold the product, doesn't it?

No wonder so many women say, "Why? How could such a terrible thing happen to me?" when their husbands die.

All I can answer is, "Why not?"

Some of the women you and I have known for years are moping around claiming to be the only women in the world whose husbands have died and left them here. Some are even mad about it. Frankly, I think "here" is a pretty good place to be, and I'm more than certain you would have felt the same way had you been the one to be "remaindered." (I just made up this term for this condition of widowhood. Rather calls to mind the tables of cut-rate books in B. Dalton or Waldenbooks — the books nobody would buy at full price. A real bargain for some lucky soul, huh?)

I'm also certain that you would not have remained available on the bargain table for very long. You might have had a hard time deciding between the two obvious candidates for Mrs. Weaverhood, but like most men you would not have been single for long. Statistics prove that. Far more older women than men live alone. I almost added, "you know."

Let's look for one moment at the subject of pre-planning funeral services and such. You were most specific, probably because you had heard so much about the subject from your father. You were not as monotonous as Joe, thank heavens. As a matter of fact, you detested Joe's incessant trips to the cemetery to visit Vesta's grave because he could have put some of that thoughtfulness into caring for her while she was alive. Agreed. But you were almost comically insistent about wanting to be cremated and buried in the Beulah Cemetery. Everyone laughed when you explained your reasoning: the Beulah lots were so cheap, and the view was spectacular. You did want the ashes buried and a permanent marker. Good for you, John. None of us sat around wondering or whispering about what Old Dad would want us to do. You made that clear. I've followed your example and have the whole thing on file at Ascension Church, but I've included a postlude of *Onward Christian Soldiers* at top volume. We should have thrown that in for you.

We did have your ashes moved into Pueblo after Ascension built the columbarium, but we left the marker in Beulah. Since you always wanted an epitaph, I put on the stone the best for you I could come up with, simply, "He gave . . ." Anyone seeing the stone can finish the sentence according to their experience of knowing you. I'm proud of that. I put on all the initials after your name: M.D. and F.A.C.S. Important, to say the least.

So there's another plus for our ledger. You made those decisions and those days easier for all of us. Thanks.

When you hear *Onward Christian Soldiers* rattling the north end of Pueblo, you'll know I'm on my way.

Your loving wife,

*Fran*

❦

THERE'S MORE TO ME THAN I'VE USED YET

# II. AGING? WHAT'S THAT?

## MAKING CHOICES

Every time I seat myself in front of this Toshiba and stare at the blank screen, I operate purely from choice. The world will not change much at all because of what I do here. Certainly no gun is held at my head, no dire consequences lurk on the horizon should I choose not to write. The choice belongs to me.

How many times do we forget that basic fact of life? Our choices seem to be obligations or bad luck or "fate." Others might turn out more like good fortune or surprises.

Think back. Very little happens in our lives that did not depend in the beginning on our own decision, our own choice. Whether it concerns marriage, or job, or friendships, or wearing a sixteen instead of a twelve, the choice has been ours at one time. We drew the design.

Years ago, I told you about an older woman I met on a plane who bred fancy rabbits. That woman had a new lease on life with her rabbits — new friends, new horizons, new purpose. She had chosen bunny-culture rather than sitting around home waiting for the kids to call. But she had spent a lifetime with other choices that led up to the one I mention. Undoubtedly she had chosen in her marriage to be less dependent, therefore more self-reliant. She had chosen to enter a field that would provide a totally different challenge from her New England background.

That, I'd call world-class choosing. Big time in her life. Other choices are less spectacular yet carry equally important results. A motivator named Zeigler claims he stayed overweight for twenty years until he realized that being fat was his choice. "Insidious" is the word I want here, I think.

"Never have I put one bite of food in my mouth accidentally," he said. "All that I ate was by my own choice — every bite." More life-changing, even life-threatening, than breeding rabbits, but still a matter of choice. I need to remember that the next time I drool over the Ben and Jerry's ice cream in the supermarket freezer.

I also need to remember the "my choice" part when tempted to complain about delays in airports or snags in the book business. The choice was mine. I could have stayed home. I could have chosen to play the violin instead of writing. Fussing about the position in which we put ourselves makes little sense to those who are around to listen to us. They might well choose to be elsewhere the next time we crab about what is essentially our own choice. Notice I did not say "fault." Admitting the choices sounds bad enough.

A roomful of us listened to a woman complain bitterly about the treatment she was getting from her ex-husband. The tirade reached monumental proportions. Finally she raged, "He really knows how to push my buttons."

A quiet voice interrupted. "Of course he knows how to push your buttons. After all, he installed those buttons." Laughter didn't last long when the voice continued, "And you chose him for the job."

Point of all this pondering? Maybe considering our choices more carefully would be a good idea for all of us.

⁂

# AGEWISE AND WITTY

O nce in a while the subject for a column gets me so excited I can't
even come up with a first line. (That's my rule of composition:
Until the opening line sounds just right, the rest of the piece
hangs back in the shadows someplace.) Today's subject deserves the best
introduction the old word-processor can muster: *AgeWise*.

Out there in Portland, Oregon, an enterprising gang of seniors have put
together their own TV production company. "Gang" suits these people.
Thinking and working together, laughing and joking and creating together,
these oldsters operate more cohesively than does any ordinary committee or
team.

A guest shot with *AgeWise* beats other TV talk shows by a country mile.
The difference lies in the spirit of the programming. I wasn't there just to
peddle books. These folks "talk" about whatever means the most in their
senior lives.

Vivian Grubb's quote in the case study published for this project says it
well: "As an aging person, I join with other seniors in my desire to remain
independent and to do for myself as long as possible."

Kay Boylen explained the workings of the group when she introduced
me with a wine-and-cheese party the day before our actual taping. From
there on, you should have seen it! When Kay and I walked into the studio
— this is community cable-access television — those same gray-haired men
and women I'd met in their party clothes were all jeans and sneakers,
shoving cameras, shifting overhead lights, climbing or holding ladders,
testing sound systems, moving furniture, checking monitors. Nearly

everyone had a clipboard. Absolutely everyone had a smile, even though they were dead serious about the work they had been assigned to do. Of course they're volunteers, except for one young man from the cable company and the big boss, Tom Taylor, whose expertise keeps the show going.

On first and third Tuesdays, these people turn out shows of five regular segments, basically: health, legal-financial, how-to, reaching out, and activities. The programs are aired at various times on community cable channels throughout the metropolitan Portland area.

Certainly the volunteer crews are trained. They understand TV production in minute detail. They function in a professional manner. But it still tickled me to pieces to see bald heads gleaming under the studio lights as Art and a couple of others positioned the cameras. A sweet little soul named Alice turned into a veritable C. B. DeMille with a touch of Hitler when she waved her arms to signal time lapses and camera angles. In the sound booth, Ann worked efficiently with headset in place. The script session before starting the "roll" covered all possible subjects and priorities for the round-table discussion we would present, talking about everything from remarriage to sensible packing to studying at Elderhostel.

*Lights! Camera! Action!*

Believe me, it was a swell show.

Just ask the rest of those old goats.

❦

# CREATIVITY COUNTS!

That "voice from afar" spoke to me again last week. Not often do I get these messages, but once in a while Truth hits with the force of the spoken word, particularly words I hadn't thought of myself. You know how that goes: All of a sudden you hear yourself saying "Oh, yeah!"— and meaning it.

No world-shaking communication caught my attention, just a friendly voice saying, "Good for you, Frances, your life looks really fine in these 'senior' years. But then you always did have a knack with leftovers."

Think about that. Here we find ourselves in the phase of our lives most of us have dreaded — fearing we'll not measure up to the rest of the world's standards just because we've celebrated more than sixty birthdays. The kids are grown and have families of their own. Our life's work might have run its course. Easily we can fall into the trap of feeling worn out, useless, no longer needed. Or do we expect to spend the rest of our days collecting compliments for the good job we've done so far?

What we might fail to do is appreciate the possibilities of the leftovers of our lives. This harks back to our hostess years.

Remember those mornings after your splendid dinner parties when you opened the refrigerator to discover a dozen or more dribs and drabs of meats, vegetables, dips, celery sticks, cut cheeses, a few mushrooms, a little dressing, fruit salad, and half a can of olives? We knew then, you and I, how to put some of those odds and ends together to make at least two decent meals for the family or to fix a fine tea party for a child. This amounted to more than "making do:" Often the result tasted better than the original dish.

Looking back on these past ten years of my own life, I can see now the use I have found for leftovers. What leftovers? Just like the celery sticks and the extra chicken, I recognize now that I had stores of energy, curiosity, places I wanted to go, books I'd not taken time to read, subjects I'd never had a chance to study, like anthropology.

It has come to me gradually that any woman who's kept a family on an even keel, survived den-motherhood, and organized fund drives can most assuredly use those same skills in fashioning for herself a life filled with interest for herself and others. Just as she could dump the rice and the chicken together, add a bit of curry powder, the left-over pineapple plus the ever-present can of mushroom soup and have rave reviews for her inventive cookery, so can she mix some old skills with old and new interests and convince her world she's able to fend for herself, even when the hair grays and the upper arm tends to sag a bit.

Certainly this leftover housewife from Beulah, Colorado, cannot speak from more than her own experience, but hear this: When widowhood became the reality of my own life (one more rite of passage), I felt there still was a part of me I hadn't used yet.

Strange as this might sound at sixty-six, I have talked with hundreds of other women who felt the same way: "I've done it all for everybody else; let's see what I can do for myself and for my family on this different level."

On the other hand, if we leave the leftovers in the refrigerator, they'll wither and mold and nobody will care.

⌘

# BUT DID YOU KNOW HIS BROTHER?

Two old friends met outside the supermarket to exchange the usual good-old-boy compliments. Finally, Jack threw back his shoulders, sucked in his midsection.

"Tell me, Bob, do I look like a seventy-six-year-old man to you?"

"Nope. But I remember when you did."

Not "looking our age" bothers some of us a lot.

Others of us funnel our aging concerns in other directions. Some folks are surprised to realize that men care almost as much about looking younger as do women. They probably tried to look older during high-school years, too. Some people want to live their entire life-span appearing to be twenty-eight.

In Florida I heard about a fine, clean-living, upstanding citizen who disappointed himself one day by standing in front of a full-length mirror. "Gosh. I look really old," he said. "I'd better get rid of this paunch and get myself in better shape."

Months later he stood in front of the mirror to admire his new figure. Not Mr. Universe, but definitely improved — younger, he thought. "Good for you, George," he congratulated himself.

The next time he posed in front of the mirror he noticed a flaw in his new "persona." Baldness. Now his attention focused on his head. Can't look like a youngster with that shining pate.

So off George went to the wig shop. The clever young lady in the wig store fitted George with just the right hairpiece to take years off his appearance. She gave him the impression that he might be in line for the lead in the revival of an Andy Hardy movie. George felt he had a new lease on life because he looked so young — in the mirror in the shop.

Just as George stepped off the curb in front of the hair store, one big truck knocked him down. He lay there in pain and anger. "God!" he shouted. "How could you let this happen to me? I've always been a nice guy! I've helped people! I've tried to do the right thing! How could you let this happen?"

God's voice resounded. "George! I didn't recognize you!"

I heard that story from a minister who obviously wanted us to know there's more to be valued in our lives than trying to look young, at any age.

When we reach senior-citizenship, certainly most of us, without being morbid, do find ourselves thinking about how we want to be remembered. The sort of memories we leave behind will not depend on the color of our hair or the wrinkles around our eyes. What will matter more will be our relationships, our caring, our concern for others.

A young priest conducted burial services for an old parishioner he had not known personally. He asked if someone in the congregation would say a few kind words about the departed. No response, even after he asked several times. The young cleric was delighted to see a very old man finally shuffle to the front of the gathering.

The old man sighed, and said simply:

"His brother was worse."

Is that what they'll say about you?

ও

# NOW, WHERE . . . ?

Eyeglasses, car keys, and my purse — in that order — are driving me around the bend. There are times when I yearn for the good old days when I could neither read nor drive, and could carry all the money I needed tied in a knot in the corner of my hankie. But that was more than fifty years ago. It's been downhill ever since.

Glasses are the worst, because of the unwelcome dependence, I suppose. At first it was pride. I was a closet spectacle-wearer and left them in dark corners. In order to avoid hooking eyeglasses over my nose and around my ears in public, I carried those clever folding half-glasses — with rhinestones, no less — for reading menus and price tags. Around the house I hunted frantically for the bifocals necessary for sewing, reading, and such humdrum activities.

Better-looking glasses were suggested by my husband (whose glasses were *never* lost because he kept a pair in every room of the house). I tried plastic rims, "wires," sun-darkening lenses, and designer frames, all to no avail. No matter how much my new pair might suit my personality or flatter the shape of my face, it still required a full-blown safari before I could open the mail or dial the telephone. I need glasses that glow in the dark and have a beeper attached.

More eye make-up might have been the solution to looking better, but I couldn't see to put it on. Then when I peered at myself through glasses, the mess I'd made was atrocious, and amazingly hard to wash off.

My son Matthew, exasperated with my lost-glasses syndrome, asked me years ago:

"Why don't you hang them around your neck on that old-lady chain Dad gave you?" He had answered his own question, of course.

But I am not alone here.

Watch what happens in a group of women when someone brings out pictures of the new baby. With the precision of a ballet troupe, they reach for their glasses. Some even say, "Wait 'til I get my other glasses." That's even worse than I am!

The car keys and the purse are closely related, since the keys have a habit of descending immediately into the most remote corner of my bag, covered by empty breath-mint boxes and rumpled Kleenex. Since I've convinced myself that matching shoes and bags are no longer fashionable — and I carry only one gray slouchpouch with everything but formal evening attire — I can usually find the car keys, if I can find the purse.

The hopelessness of my case is apparent, however. In despair one day, I announced to Matthew that I was going to get contact lenses. "Great idea, Mom. Go for it! Then you'll only lose them once!"

So I'll go on hunting for a good place to keep my glasses. Maybe I'd better just hang them on my nose and leave them there.

ℰↄ

## ONE MORE CURE FOR BOREDOM

A wareness counts.

Sometimes we miss opportunities by rushing too quickly through familiar territory. A minute or two more spent on the daily paper might liven your entire day — might even start you on a new hobby if not a full-blown career as a writer of romance novels.

Right there in every newspaper in the country — except the *New York Times*, maybe — can be found a treasure-trove of material and inspiration that will brighten any day. Crossword puzzles and the bridge column could be eclipsed by the growing popularity of the telephone-response personal ads.

Take a look. Be aware.

I have in front of me a daily newspaper offering me a free ad and voice mail enabling me to make new friends, ". . . a different way to meet your match." Don't get me wrong, here. I'm not knocking this approach to friendship. If it works for some folks, more power to 'em. What I see for me is a source of story material unequaled in variety and quantity. I read these ads and make up stories, in other words. I'm better at this than at thinking up a five-letter word meaning "withered old woman."

Example: "Romantic slow dancer" sounds intriguing. He likes slow dancing, romantic dinners, country music and antique trucks. Slow Dancer stands five feet four inches, but he's outgoing, honest and tired of being hurt. Where's the girl for him?

In the next column, obviously. I picked a real dilly. Let's pair him up with another five-foot four-inch honest, sincere, caring person who's tired of being hurt. She loves long walks, country-and-western music. Says she, "If there are any honest men out there forty to fifty, give me a call."

Now we'll write the story, just for fun and practice:

"I'll get it, Mom," Grace called, heading for the kitchen phone. "It might be for me, but I doubt it. Probably a wrong number again." She put the handful of silverware on the counter. "I'll finish setting the table, Mom. Don't do it yourself. I don't want you to get too tired in this heat."

Take a deep breath, she told herself. This could be *him*. "Hello?"

The person on the line took a deep breath. "Could I speak to Grace? I mean, if she's not too busy?"

A caring person, she thought. Another deep breath. "This is Grace. I'm not busy right now," she said, grabbing the knives and forks from the fragile hands of her feeble mother in her sixties. "How can I help you?"

Breath. Sigh. "I saw you — your ad — in the paper. You sound like just the girl I'm looking for. Do you like trucks?"

Silence. Oh, hell, Fred thought, I should have asked her about Garth Brooks first. Or maybe if she likes Chinese.

"Well, yes. As a matter of fact, I have always had an interest in trucks, but I'm more interested in antique trucks like you see in museums. Trucks on the road scare me. I really don't trust truck drivers. They don't seem honest to me."

"Oh. That's very smart of you. Some of those truck drivers are really mean. You sound like a sensible woman. Would you like to go someplace where we could talk and dance slow?"

❧

## WHO RAN THE BAKERY? THE GROCERY STORE?

Well, old folks out there, have you had the big five-o yet? Has that letter arrived from the girl who sat behind you in algebra in 1942, announcing the class reunion? Have you started your diet? Begun planning your wardrobe? Reserved a room in the choice motel in the old home town? Have you even made up your mind about attending such a function? Have you contemplated which of your classmates you'd want to reunite with and which you'd rather avoid? To get right down to it, have you decided to care at all?

Fifty years used to sound like a lifetime, didn't it? No more. For about ten years in my own life, a half century has become a logical measure of time. So what if it's been that long since I walked the halls of the high school hoping I'd "run into" a certain boy when I sauntered casually past his locker? So what if five decades have slid by while I've been out in my real world looking back on tedious Latin translations and hours of study hall?

I can face facts.

My fiftieth has arrived.

I can take it.

I won't say my heart fills with pure joy, but I can take it.

Our class "agent" back in Kansas has asked for suggestions for entertainment after the banquet. You know how that often goes. Everyone has to stand up and brag about their wonderfully bright and good-looking grandchildren, then the prize is awarded to the person who came the greatest distance. Somebody might sing.

Generally, the evening boils down to sizing up the rest of the class. For those of us who never got beyond the back row of the chorus in the operettas, recalling a glorious past is a lost cause. We just hope the cheerleaders and the May Queen show up fat.

This year, however, I am submitting a suggestion for after-dinner entertainment that might be of interest to your own reunion galas, so I'll pass it on here.

Big idea: a spell-down trivia quiz about the old home town in our good old days. For example, some of my questions would be:

Who was the mayor of McPherson?

Who ran the bakery?

Where was the Maple Tree Grocery?

How many morticians in town?

Did they all have furniture stores?

Who starred on the football team?

How often did the town whistle blow? At what time?

Which theater showed *Gone With the Wind?*

What was the principal's nickname?

Which English teacher had denture breath?

Who were the soda jerks at Hubbell's?

You get the idea. Some of those same questions might apply to your own home town, your own reunion. Right now I visualize my classmates having one glorious shouting match after another as they disagree on which direction General McPherson faces on his horse over in the park.

At least, it will beat giving them equal time to carry on about their grandkids, who cannot possibly compare with mine.

಄

# III. I'VE BEEN THINKING

# SO, WHAT HAVE YOU LEARNED?

What have you learned in the past fifty years? I have been asking myself that question (occasionally — no use making an obsession of it) ever since my semi-centennial high school reunion. Surely our education did not cease at age eighteen. With or without college, we must have added something. Incidentally, "semi-centennial" just popped into my vocabulary, like semi-annual, semi-weekly, semi-precious, semi-smart.

This word-processor represents one area of learning worth considering, particularly when I can make it behave in a civil manner. Purely mechanical learning has been an integral part of all of our lives to some extent — especially in my generation. Consider what we have learned to do since the '40s:

Drive a car with no clutch.

Buy milk at the store.

Pump our own gas.

Microwave semi-meals.

Do the laundry without a clothesline or a wringer.

Throw away just about anything.

Depend on "instant."

Our post-school education covers every waking moment, when you think about it. The food we eat, the miles we walk, the hours we sit, the newscasters we believe, the life styles acceptable for a few but off limits for most of us, diseases and disabilities unheard of in our youth. It all adds up, doesn't it? We've learned a lot.

We also have learned to blame our mothers. Whatever goes wrong, ultimate responsibility lies with Mother. I wouldn't mind that so much, except my kids have learned the same thing. From toilet training to times tables, mothers have been accused of causing more trauma than anything short of the Third Reich.

In the halcyon days of yore, women's magazines were filled with fashion, food and home-decorating ideas spiced with the latest installment of a Mary Roberts Rinehart or Kathleen Norris novel. Then came the home-remedy columns and the days of "Can This Marriage Be Saved?" We all became students of psychology. Every issue of the *Readers Digest* convinced us we had been raised wrong and were doing even worse by our own offspring.

But after fifty years? Do we still go for all that stuff?

Perhaps. Let's hope we have winnowed out enough to make sense of our lives simply because we've had more time to see how life works. At least we have learned we're not unique.

One look at Ann Landers tells us the world overflows with problems like ours, or worse. Some woman in Boise who complains about her brother-in-law who picks his teeth at the table ought to meet some of my folks, we reason. Most of Oprah's guests make the Weaver family look well adjusted — boring, maybe, but well adjusted.

What have you learned in fifty years? Countless details of changing life styles from movies to music to money management. What counts the most?

☙

## MRS. LINCOLN AND JIMMY STEWART

Emerging Christmas tradition, as noted Yuletide '90: Christmas without watching *It's a Wonderful Life* doesn't count. Old standards like Charles Dickens seem to have been relegated to the back of the bus or the bottom of the charts. Jimmy Stewart and Donna Reed have taken on the American Christmas Glow. Without Jimmy and his troubles and the elevation to angelhood of his wise old sidekick, Christmas pales a bit, these days.

Channel-switchers report seeing snatches of *It's A Wonderful Life* on three or four channels at once. I don't mind. No one complains about Jimmy Stewart. Nobody really cares about Donna Reed. The story of their trials and tribulations, reminiscent of the Ghost of Christmas Past, never fail to point out to viewers the joy of living life as we find it — of appreciating the good parts instead of letting our S&L troubles get the best of us.

My reaction when Jimmy's life has plunged him to the depths of despair reminds me of that old punch line, "Aside from that, Mrs. Lincoln, what did you think of the play?"

Certainly most of us can reflect on times of our lives that would have been different had we been writing our own scripts. The it-all-comes-out-all-right-sooner-or-later or the it-wasn't-really-so-bad-after-all attitude comes through. We get this message much more clearly from *It's a Wonderful Life* than we do from *A Christmas Carol*, of course. We can see ourselves in this newer version of the same old story.

Our sympathy for Scrooge paled long ago. He should have been reported to some fair-labor-practices board. Yet we feel little concern for the wimp who perches on a stool in a freezing-cold office writing columns of figures with a pencil stub. We'd probably lecture Cratchitt about assertiveness training. We'd find some foundation to help the kid. We'd rather not concern ourselves with tired old men in nightcaps and flannel robes, or with ghosts trailing chains about the house, upsetting the dog.

Now, Jimmy Stewart dresses like your uncle, or even your younger self. Jimmy Stewart fights the daily battle of the almighty dollar and the ungrateful kids. Jimmy Stewart heads for the bridge and we're right with him. When he runs through the darkened street, Jimmy Stewart is having our own bad dreams. We live through his struggles, fight through his problems, see his side of his "rotten" life through his eyes. We've chased through those alleys in our own dreams only to waken to find the Christmas tree and loving children ready for a high old time. And we've heard some sort of faraway bells saying, "It wasn't all that bad, was it? You survived."

This did not start out to be a home-style lecture on Positive Thinking. I'd been struck by the popularity of this movie from the '40s for a number of reasons, not the least of which is the fact that we don't seem to see as many good movies like this as in past decades. And the story fits all of our lives.

At least, Donna fared better than did Mrs. Lincoln, far as we know.

შ

# GOD HELP THE QUEEN!

I really felt sorry for the Queen at Andy's wedding. Here she was, beloved monarch of all she surveys — except for an egg-thrower in New Zealand — and her mother was glaring at her. The Abbey was appropriately festive with flowers all over the place. Horses and carriages had arrived right on the dot. The guards had been properly lined up along the Mall. The clergy and guests were in their places. The singers knew the songs by heart. The Prince of Wales read from the Bible without a single mistake. Even the little kids were on their best behavior. Except for Princess Di's hat, which must have been borrowed from George Washington, everything I saw of the royal wedding on TV was just fine — an O.K. affair.

But the Queen Mother was scowling at Her Majesty. Like she had a run in her stocking or her slip showed. Once a mother . . .

Can't you imagine a scene like this? Right after they all climbed down out of the Cinderella carriages, before they filed into the church, Queen Mum might have said something like, "Well, your father and I would *never* have invited Joan Rivers!"

All through the ceremony, the royal grandma watched the sixty-plus Queen just in case she'd commit some *faux pas* that would embarrass her mother or the Empire. In that order.

Has Queen Elizabeth II ever felt like a real queen with her mother — an experienced queen — down the block at Clarence House keeping an eye on her? Is the older woman of this duo still pouting about India?

There's a message here for all of us who are mothers of middle-age "children," even if we are not royals. The message is simple: Butt out.

The marvels of medicine and our healthful life-styles are causing what I see as a longevity crisis. I use "crisis" in the Webster's definition of the word: "turning point; a decisive time, stage, or event."

My number one son looked as if he might faint when I suggested he might have a mother most of his entire life. Nobody wants to be mothered life-long. Nobody! We — especially widows — had better remember that. "Mother" can sound too much like "smother," sometimes. Certainly we'll always be a family; but we need a more equal footing than in years past.

I have great respect for the opinions of my children — when I take the time to listen. Before our middle-age offspring grow weary of having us around, we'd better figure out how to make our own fun and balance our own checkbooks. We'd better work hard at keeping our noses out of their daily lives, unless invited in.

Next time you start to say, "Your father and I always . . ." bite your tongue, lady. So will I.

Those kids know better than we do about their fathers, and about what we all used to do. After all, during these same years when I've been learning so much, my kids have been wising up, too.

I must remember that they can't really be dummies. They have such a smart mother.

∽

## AT LAST, SOMEONE TO WATCH OVER ME

There's a new man in my life. We've been going around together for several months, now, but I don't even know his name. I call him "Walter P." He hangs out somewhere behind the dashboard of my new talking Chrysler. I've never known a man so helpful, attentive, or courteous.

Walter P. cares about me. He reminds me to fasten my seat belt. He tells me when I'm about to run out of gas. He's careful about my headlights being left on. He never lets me walk away without taking the keys with me.

When Walter P. is really happy he says, "All monitored systems are functioning."

A man like that is enough to gladden the heart of any woman. Sometimes when I'm driving alone, feeling a bit lonely, I slow down and open the door, just to hear his voice. When he says, "A door is ajar," it brightens my day.

I've been tempted to test his serenity. Nothing seems to ruffle him when he says, "Your fuel supply is low." I'd like to run completely out of gas to find out if he'd be angry. "Dammit, I told you you'd run out if you weren't careful!" or something like that. Then he'd probably say "Thank you." He says "Thank you" a lot.

Voices in cars are a lot like voices in cash registers: very sure of themselves. There's never any room for argument, or discussion, even.

One of my friends has a Datsun that came fully equipped with a sexy lady who speaks with a little Japanese accent. Walter P. has a good solid midwestern accent like Walter P. Chrysler, a good Kansas boy.

It'd be fun to do some creative meddling with these voices in cars. I'd like to make a tape to slip into someone's new Toyota that would have more interesting questions and comments:

"Where do you think you're going in *that* outfit?"

"We must be in a real hurry! Late again?"

Or, "Can't you park any better than this? We're a good three feet from the curb!"

Walter P. would never talk like that to me, of course. He smooths my frazzled nerves with his milk-and-honey voice when the lid of the trunk is not tightly shut, then says "Thank you" when I slam it down.

I'm pretty sure it is he who turns on the interior lights when I start to get in and finds FM stations while I'm driving across Iowa. He's a nice guy. I'm lucky to have such a man in my life.

ᕲᕱ

# A HUNDRED YEARS, MORE OR LESS

File this under the heading of little-known facts — at least, of facts not widely recognized outside of Colorado: The summer of 1990 marked the centennial of our state capitol — the one with the gold dome we used to be able to see shining in the sun while we were still many miles south of Denver. You must recall those glorious days.

Anyway, this auspicious anniversary prompted Colorado historians to open the box that had lain in the cornerstone of our beautiful classic state house for those hundred years. The contents of that box must have been publicized, but if so it escaped my notice. I do know that a replacement collection of current Colorado interest was then sealed into the container.

Our Colorado legislator, Steve Arveschoug, invited me to submit an item to be included in the 1990 cornerstone collection. You can imagine how much that pleased a small-timer like me! I fretted for days about just what would make the most significant contribution, the most sense to persons examining the whatever in 2090. Then I thought of my Barbara Bush column.

Barbara Bush had literally thrilled me to pieces with her speech to the graduating class at Wellesley College in June. I certainly hope you remember it, too. Her emphasis on the role of women in our American family life, in the nurturing of our children and the preservation of our home life, in our traditional values, lined right up with my own feelings. Naturally, anyone who agrees with me rates no less than brilliant in my book. So I wrote a glowing heartfelt accolade for our First Lady.

I still think her best line was, "The future of this country does not depend so much on what happens in the White House as what happens in *your* house." After all these months I still choke up on that one. Consequently, my choice for submission in the cornerstone collection, 1990, had to be that column. It seemed to me to carry to future generations one of the major concerns of our time, expressed by the memorable wife of our president.

I've tried to envision those people who will open that sealed box in 2090, if the building still stands and the people are concerned with cornerstones at all. Looking back at the changes during this century, the prospect boggles the mind.

Will they still be haggling over pollution while the purple mountains' majesty fades deeper into the smog? Will those Twenty-First-Century politicians have solved the problems of the homeless, the state highway system, the new airport (yet?), the wilderness areas, the dumps, or the ever-growing population of old folks? Will the Boulder Buffaloes still be laughing about that Notre Dame touchdown called back because of clipping? Will Coloradoans live closer to the beach because California fell off? Will they still be reading the *Chieftain* in Pueblo?

We can picture the moment of bicentennial opening now, can't we?

Certainly everyone will say, "Who on earth was Frances Weaver?"

Some might even say, "Who was Barbara Bush?"

I just hope they won't be saying, "What's a family?"

&

# THE DISRUPTIVE CASTING AGENCY

Not everyone knows about the top-secret Disruptive Casting Agency. I verified its existence only recently, so I feel obligated to spread the word to the unsuspecting public about this insidious organization.

My discovery was made during a week long seminar — "Irresistible Magazine Writing" — at the Smithsonian. Five minutes after the beginning of the first session, a balding, distinguished-looking man in a three-piece suit interrupted Edwards Park's opening remarks.

"I wish to question the title of the seminar."

Mr. Park was startled. Magazine writers do not wear three-piece suits to seminars or workshops. He stared at the interrupter.

"What do you wish to question?"

"Just what is this supposed to mean? Are we to understand the magazine is irresistible, or the writing?"

"Well, I didn't choose that title myself . . ." The extraordinarily articulate Edwards Park was stammering.

"Let's get this straight. I am not a professional writer. I certainly don't need the money. I happen to be a retired attorney. My background is the precise use of the language . . ."

That went on for a week. The rest of us were furious. Every hour on the hour this person would demand attention, disrupting lectures or discussion. His preface was always the same: "With my background in the legal profession, as an attorney . . ."

When I complained bitterly, my friend Dell explained.

"That man was sent from Disruptive Casting. I have one of those same jerks in my crafts class — always telling the teacher how to do everything. Last week there was one of their women in line at my supermarket. She kept running back down the aisle for 'little things,' then couldn't find her coupons. They're all over. It's big business."

It's true. I'm sure of that. Somewhere out there is an office where abrasive people report for work every morning. A brawny woman in a Cecil B. DeMille outfit waves a riding crop and assigns jobs:

"Whitsworth, go on the historic-preservation tours and talk about your ancestors.

"Gigi, you show up late at the French cooking class.

"Marvin, you and Shirley go to the movies — explain the story in detail and tell her how it's going to end.

"Gonzales, go to Spanish 101 and talk fast."

You'll find them everywhere. Remember the homey-looking woman in the waiting room of the pediatrician's office whose kids had runny noses and ran wild while she diagnosed every other child in the place? Or the man with the big voice explaining the menu in a Chinese restaurant? Child stars from the agency are labeled "gifted" and are sent off to drive each other crazy.

The Disruptive Casting Agency operates worldwide. Now that your awareness has been aroused, you'll be able to identify more and more of its operatives. I'll bet I could get a job there myself.

⌘

# NOW, *THAT'S* A SHORT STORY!

This column never gets off the ground, never gets into the innards of this word-processor, until real excitement sets in. It shall certainly surprise my readers to know that some of my columns have been exciting to me, but the fact remains: Unless I get worked up, I don't get started. Par for the course for writers.

Today's excitement hits a new high. I've discovered "flash fiction." The term, new to me, refers to short, short, short stories. Like a page and a half.

These columns run four hundred words. Some of the stories of flash fiction are even shorter than that.

Who writes this new genre, if that's what it can be called?

Big names and no-names, but very talented people. Joyce Carol Oates, John Updike, Margaret Atwood have written shortest stories included in the collection originating at Wright State University in Ohio. The editor, James Thomas, says in the introduction to *Flash Fiction* (Norton), ". . . It is interesting to note that the public taste for brevity in fiction has fluctuated over the years. Fifty years ago very short stories could be found in magazines, but fifteen years ago it was most unusual to come across a story of under five pages in the respected magazines and literary journals of this country."

He goes on to say that "By the end of the eighties the [shorter] form had a fervent following and was now being widely published."

You know what that tells me? I haven't been keeping up. Oh, well. Now I have been introduced by my up-to-the-minute grandson, who has studied writing and literature at Stanford. He knows all about this sort of thing. He's helping me to learn.

How can anyone write a real story, a meaningful tale, in less than two or three pages? Isn't that more of a sketch? A scene? A fragment of life? How can any writer do a decent job of description, character development, plot, and all that in such a short space?

Only the best writers can, I'd say.

Let's take Updike as the example. His *The Widow* says in very few of just the right words what I have been trying to convey to women like me for the last ten years. In a simple format of "Q&A" the life style and life changes of single-at-seventy emerge with a reality and clarity seldom achieved in longer works. It starts like this:

"Q: Nice place you have here.

"A: I try to keep it up. But it's hard. It's hard.

"Q: How many years has it been now?

A: "Seven. Seven come September. He was sitting in that chair, right where you are now, and the next minute he was gone. Just a kind of long sigh and he was gone."

The story ends:

"Q: . . . Your testimony is so positive, so unexpectedly so, that we want to bring to the widest possible audience . . . uh, its great value in this era of widows, to all others who find themselves alone.

"A: You are not alone. You are not. Not."

I won't spoil it by telling the middle of the story, but think about Updike's masterful telling. He had no need to tell us details. We saw the scene ourselves. Flash fiction works.

∽

# ISN'T THAT THE OLD PALMER METHOD?

I majored in push-pulls. A lot of the kids in my class preferred doing ovals, but I prided myself in making neater pages than anyone in Roosevelt fourth grade, or, at least, in my row. Back in the thirties, penmanship mattered, neatness counted. We worked at being good writers and good spellers.

Spencerian number five. Remember that, you old fogies out there? On the day we bought our school supplies at the book store, we had to include Spencerian number five pen points. The pen might differ from our classmates', but the point had to be the same. One of my favorite pens had rainbow colors. I showed off with that one. We also had to buy our own ink to keep in our desks, ever mindful of the danger of spilling on our tablets or the textbooks crammed in there.

Now, I do not date back to those *Little House on the Prairie* days with boys sticking girls' pigtails in their inkwells. Actually, only Bessie Fairbairn had pigtails in our crowd. She's the girl who became famous when Donald Saylor pushed her off the big slide in a fit of passion and broke her arm. Then she couldn't do push-pulls at all for a while.

Almost every day I'm reminded of the importance of penmanship in our early years. The trick was to get just the right amount of ink on the pen point to write but not enough to make blots. That was disastrous — when too much ink ruined a neat page of writing exercises. We must have had blotters in our desks, too. I'd forgotten about the blotters.

Why tell you all this? The *Chicago Tribune* reported not long ago that we had had National Handwriting Day and I missed it. Didn't even know it was on the calendar. That just makes me sick. I could have had a real celebration of National Penmanship Day. What a day that could have been!

I could have made pages of push-pulls and ovals, except the challenge fades with a ball-point pen. Almost no blots. I might even have used my Mont Blanc for such an occasion. That would have made Miss Reichardt proud. She used to patrol the aisles of fourth grade, checking on our penmanship practice. Miss Reichardt cared and so did I. The real trick lies in getting the slant just so. You don't want the push-pulls straight up and down, but they cannot be lying on their sides, so to speak. Just leaning slightly to the right, and even spacing.

The ovals should list a bit toward starboard, too. Just enough to be graceful. And even. You dare not have one loop bigger than the others — spoils the whole line. Ovals depend on arm movement to be right. None of this choking the pen with grubby fist-like fingers when perfecting ovals. No drawing the circles with tight motion. No. The hand must be free to move in a flowing motion, arm comfortably resting on the desk or table.

Who cares? Almost everybody I see, these days. I spend a lot of time autographing my books for women and men of my generation. Believe me, not one day passes without at least a half dozen folks commenting, "Oh look, she's writing Palmer Method! What a lovely readable signature!"

Miss Reichardt should be proud.

## YOU WANTA SEE MY *WHAT?*

T he old lady standing at the teller's window in the drive-in bank was close to apoplexy. She might just plain explode at any moment. Her hands shook. She glared at the fortyish woman behind the glass and hollered.

You wanta see my *what?*

"Your driver's license, ma'am." The teller repeated for the third time.

"Just to cash this check?"

"For a check of this amount, that's the bank's policy, ma'am."

"Have you any idea how long I've been doing business with this blessed bank? For thirty years I've been — my husband was — my son was — I'm on the —" She was sputtering out of control.

"Yes, ma'am. I know. You have an old account number. We appreciate your patronage, but this is bank policy for this much cash."

That old lady stomped out to her car ready to bite somebody.

You know the old lady. Me.

How can this be happening, I fumed. After all these years. Then it dawned on me. *I've* been the fixture at that bank, not that poor gal in the teller's cage. Why in the world should she know me? The walls, the floors, the old pens on the customers' counters have been there all of my banking years. Not the people.

From the bank I made the rounds of the utility companies in Pueblo, arranging new hookups for a condominium. None of those young clerks knew me, either. Each required a deposit. "Now, wait!" I wanted to scream. "I'm an old-timer in this place!"

This happens to most of us old-timers once in a while. Part of growing old gracefully is accepting the fact that we've outlasted the bank tellers, retail clerks, and pharmacists who were our friends. The old gang has retired. These new folks don't know us even though we were doing business at that counter before they were born. All of us are more comfortable being "waited on" by someone who knows our name.

In one of the Pueblo supermarkets, there's a clerk who was checking out my groceries before Matt was born. Matt is twenty-seven now. I still like Connie to check out my groceries. She won't demand my driver's license. But that's the exception that proves the rule.

According to behaviorist B. F. Skinner, old persons are often looked upon as crotchety, boastful, boring, demanding, arrogant. He claims we must all be on our guard not to fall into the same sort of behavior in our own senior years. Well, maybe nobody at his bank has asked to see B. F. Skinner's driver's license. Or maybe he's better at remembering that everyone he meets hasn't been around as long as he has.

That's what I'm going to try to do.

❧

# JUST WAIT 'TIL YOU SEE MY VIDEOS!

My new chosen avocation, videography, comes up to most of my expectations these days. The camera doesn't weigh me down. The cassettes are handy to carry and load. Charging the batteries takes little time and can be done in any motel, or on board ship, for that matter. The autofocus part functions almost miraculously. Color, fine. Sound, extraordinary.

Best of all, this gem from JVC has a readable, easily understood manual. The diagrams make sense. The language is housewife-friendly. So far, no problem has arisen that couldn't be solved by carefully studying the instructions. Except for one small item — I'll take that back; except for one major item. I plan to write to the manufacturer about this.

*Attracting an audience.* You probably won't believe this, but the manual has not one page, not one word, about how to persuade friends, relatives, or total strangers in national parks, or members of your ladies' club or even your local librarian, to attend a viewing of your videological triumphs.

I have found only one sure way to convince anyone to watch my pictures: Shoot at least ten minutes of somebody else's grandchild. Then you know you'll have one taker when you smile prettily and announce, "Well, it's all set up. Who wants to see Erma's dear little Christopher?"

But that's it. If you thought Erma would then suggest seeing, or tolerate your showing, superb scenes of the Oregon coast, forget it. Not even Oregonians fall for that one. Not without their own grandchildren or their dogs.

Surely we camcorder enthusiasts can discover some way to establish an audience — to generate enthusiasm for our new-found skills. After all, my pictures have improved immensely. I'll admit that. Not since last January at Elderhostel in Georgia have I forgotten to turn off the machine while boarding a sightseeing bus. That footage was a little sloppy, especially when viewers don't relish the humor in shots of the feet of strangers and the backs of the seats on the bus.

I find the recorded conversations in the boarding process intensely interesting. I play a little "voice-identity" game, even though the camera work tends to bring on minor motion sickness in some cases.

Perhaps I should serve refreshments. Maybe even cocktails. Some sort of bribery apparently has to be the answer for this calamitous condition. After all, most of the loved ones with whom I choose to share my specially recorded moments have grown to depend on me for a certain amount of sustenance. It's unrealistic to expect them to sit through more than an hour of Butchart Gardens, Florida horse farms, Jekyll Island Spanish moss, temple ruins in Malta, toy stores in England, Santa Barbara Pier, burned-out Yellowstone timber, rhododendrons in Portland, and the Washington Monument without some cookies or at least some avocado dip and Fritos.

Just writing this piece has made me see the light about a lot of this.

In looking back at old family home movies from my own youth — marvelous films spliced together in one happy jumble of parades, vacations, and cousins — I've tried to recall just what attracted the greatest responses from audiences.

Nobody wanted to see them, either.

❧

## JITTERBUG RAP

I suppose rap "music" has gone out of style. That means it's time for me to try it. How about this? Does it need a tune?

*Come on you Grannies, get in the groove!*
*This old folks' world is startin' to move!*
*No more waitin' for the phone to ring!*
*No more huntin' for blues to sing!*
*You and I got plenty to do!*
*Just playin' catch-up will take a few*
*Months of practice, then we'll really swing,*
*Just like Benny or some Dorsey thing!*
*The more we sit the more we grumble.*
*You'll feel like your hind end's caught in the rumble*
*Seat of your boy friend's old Model A*
*Back in the thirties —*
*That'd be the day!*
*Forget about the old days? Not if you're smartest!*
*You can make new days — you're a new-day artist!*
*Take all the good stuff you know how to do,*
*Match it up easy with somethin' brand new!*
*Surprise all the young bucks, enlighten your kids!*
*Show you've learned more than pre-emptive bids.*
*Join a few classes, shake those tired limbs!*
*Go for a workout in broken-down gyms!*

*You'll fit right in there if you don't watch your step!*
*"Fit" is the right word if you're gonna be hep!*
*Try a new hobby, tie a new fly!*
*Climb a small mountain just fifty feet high!*
*But get out and do it! Don't sit there and rust!*
*Read a new book, help the old lady dust!*
*Walk at your leisure around the school track,*
*Then wait a few days before you try to go back.*
*Don't whine about Dentugrip, Maalox and Tums,*
*Call up your old cronies — those lazy bums*
*Sprawled 'front of TV, rotting away*
*While you're out there having a wonderful day!*

Like it? Actually, writing that took no more than ten minutes, much easier than I thought it would be. When you stop to consider it, those rap people don't look like they've spent much time holed up in a library some place. Brainless, but exhilarating, I'd say, even for an old gal pushing seventy. Try one. This could be your latest after-dinner entertainment: senior rap.

Actually, I should have included more buzzwords like AARP or Medicare, but those don't rhyme easily. What possible line could follow something about Social Security or old-age pension? How about a real rib-tickler to rap about managed competition? You could stick in something about "Hillary Clinton keeps on hintin' / 'Bout health care . . ." — but where do you go from there?

Maybe the next time I'm confronted with rap "music" from any source I'll pay more attention. I guess that old saying, "If you ain't tried it, don't knock it," applies to young folks' music as well as to the rest of their world.

⟡

# IV. ON TRAVELING

## GET THERE AT LEAST TWO HOURS EARLY

The final breakdown of our "modern" civilization will result directly from airports. Authorities around the world pontificate about just how our final "fall" might take place, but my money stays on airports. Sooner or later the entire population of every continent, maybe one person at a time, will succumb to one massive nervous breakdown and disappear into the mists of history. Because of airports.

All that'll be left for the archeologists will be a few baggage carts with wheels turned sideways and skeletons of several hundred women in line in front of a door marked only with the silhouette of a figure wearing a skirt. Beside each skeleton will be the remains of a ten-pound leather purse filled with car keys, decayed leaflets about cathedrals and prehistoric castles, and enormous plastic bottles labeled "shampoo." All of their skeleton feet will be encased in petrified Rockport walking shoes.

Research teams will announce to the press with some surprise that each of these female figures has one shoulder decidedly lower than the other, as if these women walked and stood on the bias. Speculation that this phenomenon could be connected to the piles of indestructible purses, satchels, and duffel bags will be turned over to another team of experts.

Surrounding areas littered with canvas bags marked "Jane's Travel Service" will tell the story as scientists of the Twenty-Second Century sift through leather straps, assorted metal tubing contraptions with no apparent purpose, and one primitive tower laid on the ground as if toppled by a stampede of over-wrought Italians. Sort of like after a soccer game.

The demarcation of this enormous treasure-trove of archeological trash I see as a peripheral trench extending several miles to be dug encircling the site. This trench can easily be identified by orange cones and a multitude of galvanized panels all striped diagonally with the same vivid hue, which shows no signs of fading after hundreds of years underground.

Connecting with this trench, criss-crossing the activity centers, will be enormous purple, green, red and brown signboards bearing fat white arrows pointing left, right, upward or down-slant. Words like LONG-TERM, ARRIVING, and DEPARTING might still be legible. Dozens of these panels will be unearthed along each of the long-forgotten "roads" that curve, overlap, and cross each other in patterns reminiscent of the plates of spaghetti on which many of these people apparently depended for their near-primitive nutrition.

Signs reading TAXI will be found crumpled in a huge trash concentration resembling an Etruscan burial ground topped by an astonishing collection of sledge hammers.

Absence of aircraft will mystify those who first unearth these sites. In spite of the presence of small tractor-like vehicles scattered near the boarding gates, and trucks on which MOBIL or MARRIOTT can still be made out, no sign of any flying machines will appear. Crushed computers and female remains wearing size ten navy-blue blazers might lead the searchers to expect to find at least one or two of the legendary 747s or DC-9s. But no.

The aircraft will be discovered at secondary, newer sites. Farther out of town.

༉

## SIENA LIGHT

Never have I seen such an orange sky turn to red before becoming a deep red velvet drape spread above black mountains in the west. Should anyone have shown me paintings or even photographs of such a sky, my response probably would have been, "Oh, get real!"

But this brilliance filled the sky over Tuscany this evening, turning old gray buildings a dazzling gold. Such a light made every distant building look like a medieval fortress from one of those stories about the princess waiting to be rescued.

Perhaps my strongest memory of this Smithsonian Countryside journey to this part of Italy will remain the impressions of light. Sunlight bouncing off the glorious gold dome of the cathedral, gray light of rainy days misting the hills with their rows of cedar trees, brightly lighted narrow streets in celebration of a thousand-year-old horse race that lasts thirty seconds. Sienese light. Sienese colors. Sienese continuing history.

All add up to a sense of living inside a painting — for me, anyway.

From our first glimpses of Siena perched on three hills, within fortifications older than most anything in America except the Grand Canyon, awareness of light in the public squares has contrasted with the dark of streets just wide enough for one American tourist to be passed by one Fiat. All this had registered in this head before we even started to look at paintings and churches and museums and all the rest. No wonder artists loved to paint here! Look at the light!

Through days of observing works of art through the centuries of the Middle Ages and the Renaissance I was more enlightened, myself — a poor pun but a true saying. The Etruscans back in 800 B. C. concentrated their artistic efforts on tombs and burial urns, but they became pretty good at carving figures of stone and handy at building burial vaults still being uncovered in Tuscany. With the fervor of Christianity, the Italians really set to work creating astonishing structures and beautiful paintings and sculptures.

All of Siena is a work of art. All of Tuscany ought to be declared a property of some national trust. Perhaps that has already happened, but it's true.

When you're in this glorious section of Italy, every way you turn you see some other antiquity that takes away your breath.

Peering up at the wall of a bank building in midtown Siena, we spot wonderfully real carved faces of saints and ancient scholars peering back at us.

In one small square stands a benignly frowning cardinal from the Fourteenth Century who can't fasten the buttons of his cassock over his round belly.

On street corners and in what look like American back alleys are figures and frescoes dating back hundreds of years.

The city hall out-museums any local government offices anywhere else I've been. Always with high Gothic windows to let in that extraordinary light. Marble floors, massive columns, and art everywhere.

Renaissance painters added perspective to their pictures that had not been seen in the Middle Ages. Those madonnas had flat faces and looked a bit stiff. The later Fifteenth- and Sixteenth-Century portraits emphasized the light and shadows, added an architectural dimension to the backgrounds.

Thanks to our great American institution, the Smithsonian, I appreciate that world more.

Bless you, Smithsonian. Bless you, Siena.

ぐ

# JUST TIE IT UNDER YOUR CHIN!

New Mexico is the Land of Enchantment. Louisiana is Sportsman's Paradise. Fifth Avenue in New York City is the Place Where Scarves Never Slip.

It's incredible. Women of all ages stroll, window-shop, race, trot, amble, or stride along Fifth Avenue (or Park or Madison) with scarves slung over the shoulder or around the neck in a careless, casual manner that defies gravity and looks marvelous. Their scarves stay in place, even in a high wind. Nothing looks more sophisticated, more Smart Set, more Together, than a square or triangular scarf draped around some woman who apparently doesn't know it's there.

That's it! There's the secret! These fashion plates seem to be totally unaware of that pure silk paisley wonder swinging magically with no visible means of support!

Oprah Winfrey does it on TV. She wears a basic outfit and a big scarf — almost the size of an afghan — suspended from the shoulder, over one arm. And it never seems to get in her way. It makes you wonder if she eats dressed like that. Or kisses. Or whatever. Glamorous women have always worn scarves in some romantic fashion. Swirling behind their perfectly coifed heads in an open convertible, or wrapped around sinuous hips for a tango or samba, movie stars and models make scarf-wearing seem easy.

We know better, don't we?

Wearing a scarf is one of life's mysteries, as far as I'm concerned. The surest way for me to waste forty minutes is to open that lower drawer filled with scarves while I'm trying to dress for a special occasion.

Most of the women I know run into the same problems. Call it the "Wrong Scarf Syndrome." These beauties have been gathered from brilliant displays in museums, specialty shops, craft fairs, and Filene's basement to add just the right touch to any outfit. After I finish draping myself in one or another of the collection, I look as though I have a sore throat, lead a Scout troop, or should put the wretched thing back on the piano where it belongs.

A woolen scarf won't tie in a knot smaller than a baseball. A silk scarf won't stay tied at all. Any attempt to use something as mundane as a safety pin makes holes in the material and winds up on the outside looking tacky, anyway.

Once I tied a huge woolen plaid scarf horizontally across a black skirt and sweater outfit. That looked fine except the point of the scarf covered my right hand and was totally in the way. Then when I tried to drive in this get-up, my arm was pinned to my side. That's the same almost-shawl that slid to the street in the middle of a busy intersection when I was carrying two shopping bags, a purse, and gloves I couldn't manage to put on.

So much for glamour. These scarves will make very nice wall hangings, a fine doll blanket for Miss Sarah, or maybe a good bed for someone's dog. I'm certainly not going to wear one on Fifth Avenue again.

∞

# THERE'S NO PLACE LIKE . . . NEBRASKA?

Some of you out there might not have considered vacationing in Nebraska. As a matter of strict fact, I'd bet most of you have not included Nebraska in your itinerary. Not even on the road to Elsewhere. I have news for you: You can have a good time in Nebraska, even if your Aunt Emma doesn't live there.

That sets the tone, doesn't it? You and I are going to discuss Nebraska, but we're also going to revel in the knowledge that it's not necessary to spend time only in the glamour spots of this country to find a good time. Whatever is nearest might even outshine those faraway places with the strange-sounding names.

Don't sell Nebraska short on the strange-sounding names, however. Any state sporting names like Menominee, Niobrara, Neligh and Ogallala must have more to offer than McDonald's and Sears in the Mall.

Son Matt, his wife Sherry, and I drove from Denver to Scottsbluff for a couple of speeches for the Regional Medical Center there. First surprise: an enormous center for western Nebraska complete with sports medicine, all the latest diagnostic machines, and more. Plus really nice people concerned about each other. On the way we had seen portions of the Nebraska National Forest. Really. Patches of tall pines really stand out on those rolling hills of wheat and pasture. In the same area, great limestone bluffs stretch along the horizon just as they did when the wagons came west. Scouts used those bluffs to figure out where they were going and where they'd been.

We discovered a new food in Nebraska, right in Scottsbluff. All along the road we noticed eateries called "runza." Sometimes as a place name, often as a specialty of the house. So what is a runza? Ask that question in Nebraska, they think you came from Mars.

Runza is a sandwich about the size of a sub but the filling has been baked in the bread. When the bread was baked. Original filling apparently was ground meat, cabbage and onions with appropriate spices.

For breakfast we were served "potato ends." Local chefs fry the ends cut off to make French fries. Not a bad idea at all.

We sashayed north from Nebraska to bask in the glory of Mount Rushmore in South Dakota. Another pleasant drive. Along the way we saw more buffaloes roaming and more deer and antelope playing than I have seen in sixty-plus years of touring the West.

We stopped to see the Crazy Horse Monument being blasted out of mammoth cliffs not far from those impressive faces of stone, but that will take another column.

Back to Nebraska:

Carhenge. Carhenge and Cabela's. Both are big items for a weekend among the Cornhuskers. Carhenge sits in a field along highway 385 between Alliance and Sidney. You can see it from the road. In the exact conformation of Stonehenge, old cars have been placed, front ends buried, to simulate the stones of Stonehenge. Other old cars balance on top of these, all sprayed silver.

Cabela's claims to be the world's largest purveyor of sporting goods and they have one gigantic supermarket in Sidney to prove the point. A fabulous place. Really.

Don't miss Nebraska.

❧

## CHINA: WINGDING DYNASTY

I'm going back to China, for the same reason most tourists go to China these days — just to look at what's happening there. Much of our world I have not seen yet, but a return to China after four years seems more important than does learning to get around in Paris or Brussels, or exploring the Outback of Australia. Those places will wait. China will not.

When I was there in 1981, Peking (Beijing) was an austere city populated by millions of people in dark blue pajama suits riding bicycles. I thought something was wrong with my Polaroid because the pictures were so drab. Then I realized there were no colors to photograph in Peking, except for the neon sign at one restaurant. Peking was like a lithograph of other places; a gray, black, and dirty-white portrait of life. They tell me much of that feeling is changed, now, and one of the greatest changes is the color. The uniformity of dress of the people is disappearing. Does this indicate that communist uniformity of thought — of life style — is also on the way out?

Outside Peking, in the communes, we watched as many as fifty people with hoes, rakes, shovels, and buckets working in fields of fewer than five acres. We saw grain thrown on the roads to be "threshed" by passing busses and trucks — primitive farming by our standards. One loudmouth Californian on our bus pontificated about such labor:

"All they need here is one good tractor."

So when you put one of these Chinamen/women on a tractor with a plow, what are the forty-nine other workers going to do? How're they gonna keep *them* down on the farm? Or will they start manufacturing Chinese Toyotas?

That's the fascination with China today. The government is trying to leapfrog that gigantic country with a billion people into the Twentieth Century. Already, communist restrictions on private ownership and profit-making are being relaxed. Can communism survive, or will the entire nation be turned upside down? Will personal freedom follow westernization? That's a staggering thought.

One of the delights of visiting Shanghai was an acupuncture-style massage administered by a grinning barber while I sat bolt upright, fully clothed, in a turn-of-the-century barber chair. Now, that hotel probably has been replaced by an American-style tourist trap complete with sauna and hot tubs. Next will come Pizza Hut and Kmart.

A better life for the Chinese people is an admirable goal, of course. In the process, however, what happens to the venerable Chinese culture built on centuries of Oriental wisdom?

China is the oldest continuous civilization in the world. Will the Chinese chuck it all in order to catch up with those of us who have learned to drive ourselves into neuroses surrounded by gadgets that buzz, ding, whir, spin, and make funny pictures?

I'll let you know when I get back.

വ

# WE'RE OFF TO SEE THE CRETANS

Summer sneaked up on us this time, didn't it? Seems only last week we gathered for Christmas. I gave Sarah her passport for Christmas. Now that Sarah has blossomed into a lovely fourteen-year-old, the time has come for us to travel together, as I have done, more or less, with her brother and cousins. We have chosen Greece for this excursion. And suddenly summer is upon us. Time to get ready to greet the folks in Athens, on Crete and Rhodes.

We won't be gone long — ten days in July. Sarah has been reading up on the Greek Islands when she has had time during her busy year editing the yearbook and knocking down "A"s. Now we must get to the basics of planning travel abroad. You might find the checklist we're using to be helpful in your own summer plans.

1. Read ahead. Browsing through the travel guides in the bookstores gives us impressions of the nature of our trip. Choose to buy only one guidebook to carry along. My own preference is the American Express series because it is concise, compact and complete. Pocket-size. I see no need to lug a heavy book with pictures of what I might see, when I'll be handling my own luggage most of the time. Carrying my camera and extra film will provide for pictures. The convenient, easy-to-read Amex book includes walking tours of Athens and all that.

Reading should include research about food. Besides something wrapped in a grape leaf, what else should we expect on Greek menus? A visit to a Greek restaurant ought to be on our agenda before we leave Colorado, or fly from New York.

2.   Xerox. Sarah and I should have photocopies of our passports and all travel documents before SwissAir whisks us away. We'll make enough copies to trade. I'll carry copies of her stuff, she can carry copies of mine as well as her own, just in case we get separated from some purse along the way.

Copies of our airline tickets and the itinerary prepared for us by American Express will be in our folders, as well as the "permission statement" that says it's O. K. with Sarah's parents that she travels with me and makes me responsible for any medical care that might pop up. More often than not, a photocopy of such documents suffices without risking losing or mislaying the original.

3.   Pack light. We always say that, don't we? I recall being in Greece early in my globe-trotting days, seeing all sorts of great blouses, cotton skirts, and such I'd love to wear right there, but my luggage was too crammed full of my own clothes to squeeze in another pair of sandals, even. Besides, I had spent 'way too much money on clothes to take along, which weren't half as suitable as were local products. This time I hope I know better and leave luggage room for *their* clothes.

4.   Extras. Extra film, extra glasses, extra watch, extra comfortable shoes, extra traveler's checks.

Certainly I'll carry along the video camera. Maybe even get some pictures of the topless beaches — with the zoom lens, of course.

We'll have a good time, Sarah and I. This will be our own experience, which we shall share with each other for the rest of our lives. Then one day Sarah's mom can take one of Sarah's kids on a special outing.

Grandmothers like that.

૭૩

# THE ATTACK OF THE KILLER RIGS!

Brace your feet! Here comes another what's-the-world-coming-to column. At least I'm having that kind of a day so far.

Driving from the Ocala Hilton (maybe my favorite hotel) to absolutely my favorite airport — Tampa — seems like the best way to start the day. Not so. Headed south on I-75 I had the living daylights scared out of me by some fool eighteen-wheeler maniacs playing Florida Interstate games.

The promotion for a local newscast would be, "Crime on Florida's Interstates." I missed the newscast, but that wouldn't have made much difference. I had a plane to catch. Just picture this:

About 5:30 a. m., an hour before daylight, I concentrated on my own business in a Hertz Mercury Cougar two-door, white. The speed limit on I-75 is now sixty-five miles an hour. I exceeded that only slightly when I passed a great big truck. Back in the right lane, I slowed to less than sixty-five and settled in for a two-hour drive.

Suddenly my world filled with enormous transport trucks. One driver who was tailgating me had his lights flashing and a huge spotlight on me and my Cougar. In front of me, almost close enough to touch, pulled another big rig blinking his brake lights in my face. Simultaneously, two more trucks positioned themselves in the left lane, hemming me in. Not passing. Just hanging in there.

It took a minute or two to realize that this does not conform to my concept of a regular traffic pattern. When the guy behind first started the flashing lights I thought maybe my headlights weren't on, or perhaps he'd spotted a cop on his radar. But he kept right on with the lights and his gigantic spotlight. At seventy miles an hour!

These fools are playing some game of their own, I first thought. But boxed in the middle as they sped along that straight stretch of highway, with no exits in sight, sat one white two-door Hertz Mercury Cougar manned by one terrified Colorado housewife. The bullies in the left lane seemed to take turns swerving their trailers in my direction. These apes wanted to force me off the road! It was a clear message.

I'm dead, I thought, and nobody will ever know what happened here. They'll assume I fell asleep at the wheel. My sister will tell my mother I never was a good driver. Hertz will sue my kids. I should have gotten all the bills paid before I left home.

Now I realize why I've been advised to have a car phone. Nine-one-one would've come in handy right here. I couldn't even call my family to let them know of my ignominious end: scared into a Florida ditch by some hopped-up birdbrains entertaining themselves by terrorizing old ladies in rental cars in the dark.

For lack of a better idea I began to slow down. Of course, I couldn't put on the brakes. That redneck behind me would see the brake lights and speed up. He'd just as soon run right over me. So I took my foot off the gas a little at a time, gradually slowing to less than sixty.

They stayed right there with their stupid game for what seemed an eternity, then moved on like a pack of wild dogs tired of worrying a rabbit.

Beware.

છ૭

# THE ROVER GIRLS ON TOPLESS RHODES

A couple of Gibson Girls in Gay Nineties bathing costumes would not have been any more conspicuous.

The sky was clear, the water an unbelievable sea green shading into deepest blue. Visible on the horizon was the mountainous coast of Turkey. In close-order rows along the beach were thousands of umbrellas and lounge chairs. And there we stood, wearing our standard one-piece swim suits — two middle-aged women on a topless beach.

My friend the professor and I were on Rhodes, a stunning semitropical Greek Island which is the Mediterranean Mecca for northern Europeans, mostly sun-worshipers. All day long they lie there grilling themselves to a golden turn, clad in nothing more than a G-string. We were overdressed, to say the least.

We might just as well have been wearing one-piece black woolen Jantzens with red diving girls on the skirts. Maybe we would have looked a little better without the shoes. Hot sands and rocky beaches of other islands prompted us to sport Chinese slippers — the ones that look like "Mary Janes." The professor had her Gertrude Ederle swim cap, which didn't do a lot for the image, either.

One glance up and down the beach made it chillingly clear: We had the only covered bosoms on the whole beach, a beach that stretched for at least two miles. In forty years of practice, my gynecologist did not examine as many bare breasts as we saw on that beach in one hour. Those sauna-weary Scandinavians are the least self-conscious people I have ever seen.

My first feeling was outrage: Have they no shame? Then I tried to be cosmopolitan — cultural folkways are of interest to world travelers, I told myself. Then I remembered a class in comparative anatomy, but it was nothing like those girls parading on the sand. When I spotted women my age and older who had also shed their modesty, I gave up. Too bad they didn't.

There are many expressions about being in the minority. "Bastard at a family reunion," and such. We felt that much out of place among those nearly naked beauties, but we persevered, determined to get a tan.

That out-of-place feeling paled soon afterward when we found ourselves a part of the backpack set. But that story will have to wait for another time.

∽

## NOTHIN' COULD BE FINER

We must have been about half-way to San Francisco when I went into the diner for lunch. On the train, sharing tables is the order of the day. I eased into the seat across from a bright-looking little kid with his dad. Something about being a grandmother makes us feel that we have to say cutesy things to any child, as if we have to prove our harmlessness right off the bat.

I grinned at this youngster, making some inane remark about the fun of eating lunch on the train.

Bright brown eyes stared at me.

"How much *are* you?"

"I'm sixty-six. How much are you?"

"Four."

That's how Dylan and I got acquainted while Dylan's father sputtered about not asking ladies about their age. The rest of our lunch time passed pleasantly, discussing the passing scenery of Edwards Air Force Base and rocket launchers as well as the scenic California coast on the other side of the tracks. We also passed great fields of vegetables, but we were going so fast that neither Dylan nor I could tell the broccoli from the cabbages.

Somehow, train riders carry on conversations more easily than do fellow passengers on planes. Probably because we're not strapped in — not limited to the person in 23C while wedged into 23B ourselves. Talking much to the guy immediately beside me invariably cricks my neck. Dylan and I could talk a lot at lunch, then wander off to the observation car or back to our own seats to chat or read or doze — whatever.

Whenever time permits, I take the train for this and other reasons. Not being strapped in feels good, once in a while. After riding from Los Angeles to Portland, Oregon, I astonished myself with the variety of conversations I recalled with other passengers.

The gentleman who had started his journey in Fort Lauderdale talked a lot about trains, and about the people he'd met. He also talked about his insurance business and changing jobs even though he's over fifty. I found that fascinating, since my life seems at times to be managed by insurance. I'm sick of it, too.

The couple from Paradise, Montana, explained sheep-raising as we hurtled past pastures where grazing sheep seemed to have been arranged to add to the scenery. This man also recounted to his wife's delight the details of his job in a firm producing railroad ties. This hunk could handle from three hundred to five hundred ties per day, each weighing over three hundred pounds. How many he moved depended on how much he chose to earn that day. I really couldn't believe he lifted that much weight for hours on end, but I didn't question him — not with those muscles. Nobody argues with that guy.

One pleasant younger woman sat beside me in the observation car as we crossed a snow-covered mountain pass in Oregon. Spectacular. At one point, at least a dozen elk stood calmly watching as the train roared by and everyone on board grabbed for cameras and camcorders and missed the shot.

I did not record that conversation, but you can imagine the words.

Amtrak talk: A leisure-time bonus at any age.

❧

## WHAT'S SO GREAT ABOUT MINNESOTA?

The leaves turned in Minneapolis today. We might spot a few green ones in sheltered places, but those great green carpets beneath our plane as we landed on Thursday will have become bright yellow sprinkled with red and orange as we take off on Sunday. There are just enough hardwoods in Minnesota to spark up the fall gold with scarlet and amber. Great.

Of course, Minneapolis can well boast of one of the finest "downtowns" in the country in any season. I stood on the ninth floor of this Hyatt Regency gazing out at tennis courts, fountains, a greenway where strollers kicked aside the yellow leaves, and marveled. This is the center of the city? Close. With skyway walkways connecting stores, hotels, business buildings and the civic center, getting around mid-city is even better than Dorothy on the yellow brick road.

Notice: I have not had time to explore the brand-new Mall of America or revisit the joys of St. Paul, but I rave on as if the Chamber of Commerce had just offered me a job. I'll have to confess how much I have enjoyed Columbus and Houston in the past week, but today my sun shines on Minneapolis.

On our way to an interview on channel 11, KARE, my host and I passed the new sculpture garden.

"We're proud of that," he said. "Not many cities have their own sculpture garden apart from the museums. This one looks really good from the freeways. We like that."

Along those freeways, Minnesotans have plenty of those car-pool lanes forbidden to single drivers in cars. Two or more per car allows use of the "sane lane." Isn't that a good name?

More incidental news of Minneapolis: General Mills has been forced to cancel its guided tours of Betty Crocker's kitchens. Why? Corporate espionage. Imagine that! No more can groups of school kids or housewives watch the astonishing operation of Betty's staff because of spies from Pillsbury or Sarah Lee or who knows where. What's to know about making brownies? Plenty, it seems.

Even worse, all of the big red spoon signs directing traffic on the General Mills campus have been stolen.

My sojourn among these Scandinavian wonder-workers was prompted by the annual Senior Options Expo. Thousands of older folks thronged to the convention center for two days of seminars, entertainment, and information. Everyone seemed to be in a good mood. And the place was alive with volunteers.

My host, one charming young man named Scott Winter, claims there are always too many volunteers for Minneapolis events. Can you imagine that?

"Don't bring your convention to this town," says Scott, "unless you know you'll drive the chairman of volunteers crazy. We consistently have more volunteers than we need. Everyone in Minnesota wants to help."

Why? Why not?

Keynote speaker for this Expo was Sally Jessie Raphael. She gave a right good speech. Much more down-to-earth than I expected. However, her most enthusiastic applause followed her announcement that her husband is a Norwegian born in Minnesota.

That counts in this town.

Minneapolis, thank you.

ℰℐ

# SMALL WORLD DEPARTMENT

I did not recognize Cape Cod. That should not come as a surprise. Headed for a district meeting of the American Business Women's Association at Falmouth, Massachusetts, I told myself I'd be in familiar territory. After all, our family had spent a week on Cape Cod. Of course, that family excursion took place in the summer of '36.

No doubt about the year, here. I can remember that because that was the first Buick we had with jump seats — '36. On the way back to Kansas Dad took us out of the way up into Canada so we could see the Dionne Quintuplets. That *really* marks the date.

We saw lots more than that on that vacation, but Cape Cod and the Quints mark the time for me.

What looked so different? How could Cape Cod change? There's not that much room. Well, it did seem more crowded, but I didn't get all the way out to Provincetown so I cannot say for sure. I can remember Dad complaining about the strange road marking and the traffic. That hadn't been remedied, but now I was the driver. Being the queen of the U-turns, I set new records just trying to find the hotel in my rental car.

One word in defense of myself on those roads: Almost anyplace else you come close to an ocean, you can see it. Like driving to the mountains, you know where they are and generally which way you're going. Cape Cod is no more than a narrow string of land between two enormous bodies of water, but you can't see the water from the road. Eerie. You know there's water and beaches and all that, but the highways run right up the middle in dense forests. You can't see the ocean for the trees. And all the trees look alike. No wonder I was lost! After nearly sixty years, I could not locate the Atlantic Ocean!

But this was spring. I had seen the Cape only in summer. That astonished me even more. Azaleas bloomed. Dogwoods flowered. I thought for a minute they'd left me off at the wrong airport and I was somewhere in the South. Ornamental crabapple trees laden with bright pink petals stirred in the breezes and colored the countryside. The gutters along the main street of Falmouth were drifted full of flower petals. I never saw such a thing!

Then came one more astonishment, a small-world sort of discovery. Just beyond the pre-Revolutionary square in Falmouth, Massachusetts, I found myself on Katherine Lee Bates Road. That stopped me cold right there. Katherine Lee Bates was a distant cousin of my mother-in-law. (Her mother was a Bates.) Katherine Lee Bates is also being celebrated and memorialized in my home state of Colorado this year. You know why, probably.

One hundred years ago, Katherine Lee Bates, spending the summer in Colorado Springs, took the arduous journey to the top of Pikes Peak. Instead of simply saying, "That was nice," Ms. Bates sat down and wrote *America the Beautiful.*

In Colorado we are proud of amber waves of grain and purple mountains' majesty. So far away on Cape Cod, I was proud to be reminded of my home town in *her* home town.

☙

# AROUND THE WORLD, COME HELL OR HIGH WATER!

People die on cruise ships. Passengers, I mean. The brochures never mention this, of course, but it is a fact of the Good Life: The longer the cruise, the older the crowd. Some of the fun-seeking oldsters just don't survive.

My friend Sydney was on a long cruise last year when three passengers checked out before the end of the trip.

One old guy had a heart attack in the pool and could not be revived.

Another tumbled over the railing of the main staircase between the promenade and Atlantic decks and died. He appeared to have a drinking problem.

The third death was a man who had the bad judgment to die in the wrong room. His wife was in the beauty salon at the time. The other lady involved was embarrassed, to say the least, but the social staff took care of the matter with luxury-cruise style. They put his clothes on him and carried him to another corridor before they notified his wife about the problem.

Cruise personnel are always thoroughly and efficiently trained for such emergencies. After all, what better way to go than in the lap of luxury? Deck chairs in the sun, dancing every night, excellent room service and entertainment. Mah jongg and cribbage and bridge tournaments. Midnight buffets. Heaven!

On the most recent cruise I enjoyed, they tell me two people died. There was a lot of conversation on board about Mr. Morton after Mrs. Morton died from a bleeding ulcer — and no wonder.

The Mortons were traveling in real style. They had at least a suite, if not a penthouse suite. This means they had paid between forty and fifty thousand dollars per person for this ninety-day "vacation."

But Mr. Morton had promised to take her around the world in style, and he meant it.

A helicopter took the ailing Mrs. Morton and her husband to Singapore just at six o'clock one Friday evening and the entire complement of passengers and crew were out on the decks to watch. The only person disturbed by the procedure with the helicopter was the rabbi, because nobody came to six o'clock services. They were all out on deck.

"Better they should be praying," he told me.

Two days later, the captain confirmed the latest shipboard rumor. Mrs. Morton had not survived, and Mr. Morton would be rejoining the ship at Sri Lanka. He had been flown to Singapore from Malaysia.

Sympathy for the poor distraught man ran rampant. Late one night, just out of Sri Lanka, we ran into poor Mr. Morton in the night club. He joined us gratefully for a drink. We talked. Rather, he talked. We listened.

"I decided I'd just come on back and finish the trip," he said sadly. "I think they're gonna refund part of Margaret's fare. They goddam well better!"

We were all staring at him. He could see the question in our eyes. "I had her cremated. Brought her back on board, too. She's in a nice Chinese jar on my dresser. After all, I promised her a trip around the world . . ."

I wonder if he took her to the Captain's farewell dinner?

∽

# ONE OF THE SIGHTS IN OUR NATION'S CAPITAL

Special communiqué from Washington, D. C.:

I saw him! And he saw me, no mistake about that. I was standing there minding my own business at the intersection in front of the Connecticut Avenue entrance to the Museum of Natural History. He was riding down the avenue in an extended Cadillac limo, headed for the National Gallery of Art.

I was alone. He was with a dozen or more cops on motorcycles, several carloads of Secret Service men, and Nancy.

Even at ten paces and thirty miles an hour, that presidential smile is extraordinary. His wave was downright enthusiastic. I waved giddily at him, of course. Then he beamed at me — standing there on the curb. Nancy didn't seem to notice. but she probably has a lot on her mind.

What an addition for my Famous People page in my bulging scrapbook! I've already recorded the time I shook hands with Will Rogers when I was five and the six-word conversation I had with Cary Grant. I wrote a long paragraph about taking a picture of the Pope since the snapshot needed explanation of the red speck in the sea of heads — to remind myself about the red biretta he wore that day.

But maybe I'd better put this recollection in the Washington pages. They're more interesting, and more important. Starting with the capitol, now half hidden behind scaffolding, the Mall never fails to make me feel like a seventh-grader absolutely awed by the splendor of the buildings, the height of the Washington Monument, and the serenity of the reflecting pool in front of the Lincoln Memorial. Across the Tidal Basin, the Jefferson

Memorial seems the classiest of all — perhaps because you can see straight through it — and he looks so dignified, so aware of architectural perfection. The newest, the Viet Nam Memorial, is stunning in its simplicity, astonishing in the silence of the people who walk slowly past the thousands of names inscribed there for posterity.

Here is one notation from the Washington pages in my scrapbook when I was there last spring:

"Certainly we would visit the Iwo Jima monument. The morning — late May — was misty, cool, overcast. Those bronze Marines were dripping dark 'sweat' from the fog, straining to force that flagpole into a rocky hilltop. On the terraces around their immortalized comrades, real Marines, 1985 Marines, prepared for the Tuesday evening sunset formation. Drums and bugles. Files of bright young men crossing, strutting, tooting, marching, laughing, regrouping. My son the ex-Marine, his family, and I stood transfixed. *The Stars and Stripes Forever* hit the air like *wow!* We held hands and cried."

That's Washington. That's America.

⁓

# V. MY SPECIAL WORLDS

ONE FOOT ON EVERY ICE FLOE

# WHAT'S A KITEFLYING WIDOWED GRANDMOTHER DOING WRITING A WEEKLY NEWSPAPER COLUMN?

W hat's a wandering widow from a little mining town in the West doing in a space like this — on the features page of *The Saratogian*? Such a question is intensely interesting to me, since I ask it about myself.

There is a certain cockeyed logic to the answer. It's almost a full-circle story: My picture appeared on these pages once before — in 1978, my first year as a kiteflier-in-residence for the Conference of Women Writers at Skidmore. Being a kiteflier-in-residence is a relatively rare occupation, so I was interviewed and photographed as the kiteflying grandmother — local curiosity of the week — twelve years ago.

That was the beginning of my writing career and my first trip to upstate New York. Like most Westerners, I pictured New York as one giant slab of asphalt. Saratoga Springs and the Skidmore campus were a new world, and I was entranced.

Two years and several *Vogue* articles later, I was suddenly a widow with grown children, time on my hands, choices to make, and a point to prove. I've long been convinced that older women who find themselves bored or lonely have mainly themselves to blame — particularly those who, like me, had stuck to the traditional housewife role.

A woman owes it to herself, I insisted, to develop new skills, expand interests, and broaden her own horizons in preparation for refurbishing the empty nest. I even made speeches to ladies' groups:

"A woman who has no interests of her own is of no interest to anyone else," and so forth. I heard myself use phrases like, ". . . avoid stagnation of middle years." A lot of smart talk.

In 1980, Someone Up There called my bluff: "If women in their fifties and sixties can do so much, let's see you prove it!"

So here I am, happily writing columns for the Pueblo, Colorado, *Chieftain* and for this newspaper in my adopted home base in the Adirondacks. The first step was to locate myself, part-time, in this area. Nobody in my home town was ready to believe l was dedicating my life entirely to writing. Not at my age. Certainly, I had time to play bridge, run committees, make jelly for bazaars, fly kites, and be the "mayor" of Beulah as I always had done. A return to college was the only answer.

My bachelor's degree was almost forty years old. Time for an overhaul. Even my mother understood my moving away to go to college. I chose Adirondack Community College.

My youngest grandchild and I started school on the same day — kindergarten and college. She's half-way through seventh grade and I'm not a sophomore yet, but that's all right. I've studied creative writing with Jean Rikhoff, taken anthropology and Spanish, and discovered column-writing, which I enjoy.

The magic of the North Country has had its way with me. I now live half-time at Saratoga Springs and boast to the folks back home about the glories of SPAC, the Adirondacks, Lake George, and Ben & Jerry's French Vanilla.

A girl like me can have a good time in a space like this.

ↄↄ

# THE MILLIONAIRES' CLUB? YOU BET!

Who talks more about Elderhostel than I do? Almost everybody these days. Any time you find a crowd of wide-awake, interested and interesting people of my age (I'm still sixty-six), the topic of conversation turns to Elderhostel. One week of college courses in a live-in situation offering extraordinary opportunities for studying what we had no time for in our child-rearing, career-building years. Add to that extremely reasonable prices with astonishingly companionable people. Why not?

Most recently I participated in Elderhostel on Jekyll Island, Georgia. This fit in beautifully with a book and speaking tour I had in Florida. I could spend a week listening to someone else talk. What a relief.

Jekyll Island lies off the coast of Georgia just above Florida. I had heard of Sea Island and its fabled resort, The Cloister, but Jekyll had only a vaguely familiar ring. What a place that turns out to be, and what a history!

Three islands comprise the Golden Isles, the two I've mentioned and St. Simon's. First of all, picture huge *Gone With the Wind*-type live oak trees festooned with Spanish moss. Lots of water everywhere, open rivers and the ocean, of course, but marshes crossed by causeways. Drawbridges allow passage of shrimp boats and pleasure craft, and (in days gone by) some of the greatest private yachts in the world.

At the turn of the century, Jekyll Island belonged entirely to The Club. Financiers of our world — the Morgans, the Goulds, the Rockefellers — owned this club and the island. They spent winter months in seclusion here with their yachts and their families and their croquet mallets. They hunted wild boars and played golf. The clubhouse still stands in restored glory, operated now as a Radisson hotel. Some of the "cottages" are open for tours. This place makes *Lifestyles of the Rich and Famous* look glitzy and tasteless. Robin Leach, eat your heart out!

We Elderhostelers didn't stay at the club, but we had more than acceptable accommodations at Comfort Inn. We didn't play croquet, although we watched hotel guests who did. Instead, we had our three courses from Mercer University: "Man's Quest for Meaning" with a philosophy professor, "Coastal Georgia History," and other local studies including, "Dynamics of the Barrier Islands" and "Relationships in Art Forms, Poetry and Dance." The men in the bunch enjoyed the courses, particularly the poetry and dance, much to the surprise of their wives.

Our field trips enriched my appreciation of the area. Any native Kansan never gets over the abundance of water in a place like this. And the birds! I walked the wide hard beach every morning before class just to watch the birds. Exploration on my own took me to Christ Church on St. Simon's Island, which deserves a separate column. The history deserves more than that.

Most of all, enrichment came from the other hostelers. We had a really good time. Some were first-time. Others had attended dozens of these sessions. Some were spending the winter in warmer climes going from one Elderhostel to another. At those prices, you can't find a better way to see the world.

I don't work for Elderhostel, but it certainly works for me.

ↁ

# THAT WORKS FOR ME!

Writers write about writing and other writers when they cannot think of anything else to write about."

Maybe that's true, but once in a while I have so much to say about writers and writing I cannot *not* say it. After all, plumbers talk about faucets and drains, stockbrokers talk about all sorts of mysterious subjects, car dealers certainly talk about new models, and farmers carry on *ad nauseum* about crop failures. Once in a while, I enjoy discussing my line of work, too.

Generally this compulsion takes hold of me in July after the Santa Barbara Writers Conference. Each year that event becomes more important on my calendar. Each year I learn more about the craft I claim to practice. Each year something special happens for me there.

Writers for centuries have made a fetish of referring to their trade as "the loneliest," attempting to construct some sort of mystique around their chosen field. Readers love to picture some desolate soul isolated from the ordinary outside world in order to create deathless prose or heart-rending poetry for the ages to ponder.

Life stories of Melville, Poe, and others fit right in with the tragic ends of Van Gogh or Mozart — great artists whose devotion to the creation of beauty and truth brought desolation to their lonely lives.

Allow me to let you in on a secret: Far outnumbering those long-suffering writers who give their all for their art you can find healthy, happy, well-adjusted people who write all sorts of good stuff without even consulting a therapist or hiding out on a mountain-top.

The crowd of three hundred or more writers at Santa Barbara might have included a couple of certifiable nuts, but the vast majority write because (1) they enjoy it, (2) they think they are pretty good at it, (3) they have something they need to say. In the workshops and during breaks they find an audience empathetic to their attempts and advice from experts who love writing, too. They trade horror stories about agents and publishers but they also trade wondrous tales of success.

How does a writer measure success? Of the thousands of writers writing all sorts of readable fiction, non-fiction, poetry, thrillers, mysteries, biography and cookbooks, only a handful will "make" the best-seller lists of the *New York Times* or *Publishers Weekly.*

What they create might be fine. The stories they tell could be even more engrossing than the latest Stephen King or Sidney Sheldon. Their styles could very well entertain or enlighten the audience more than more famous authors' styles do. But — just as there's room at the top of the NBA for only so many Michael Jordans or Charles Barkleys — much of the best out there never hits Big Time. So be it, say I.

Recognition of this fact of life about writing grows with each Santa Barbara Writers Conference. Instead of narrow focus on producing a show-stopper to make millions and be translated into seven languages, writers I know concentrate more and more on the individual effect. They focus on the reader: one good book, however "small," that touches readers who care.

That works for me.

&

# OLD FRIENDS? NEW FRIENDS?

*riendship, friendship, what a perfect blendship!*

Where that lyric came from or how long it's been hiding in the back of my head I cannot say. Seems to bring with it the voices of Bing Crosby and Bob Hope, doesn't it? Like many other long-neglected rhymes, this one has been spinning in my mind again. Ah, the windmills of our minds.

Traveling as much as I do, these days, I find myself doubly blessed with friends. Not just old friends, although in our sixties we have learned to appreciate the values of lasting friendships. Almost every day brings a new friend, too. That's a bonus to the writing life I never expected.

Last week we could have labeled "Colorado Week." That was a dilly. I had the great pleasure of signing my new books at the ultimate bookstore of America, the Tattered Cover in Denver. Friends I have known for twenty years and more showed up to help me celebrate this milestone in my still-fledgling career as a writer. Members of my family were there too.

I'll tell you something I didn't intend to rave on about when I sat down to face this machine: Now that I have signed my own books, made a little speech at the Tattered Cover in Denver, I think I know how an amateur golfer feels at Pebble Beach, or a first-time player at Wimbledon. Well, perhaps not *that* much, but close. At any rate, friends made the event more special.

While in Denver I made a new friend, too. Three, to be exact. My stops there included Channel 9, KUSA, for an interview. I enjoy those talk-show hosts and their questions, particularly with a live audience. But the best part here took place in the "green room," where I waited my turn and had a chance to meet Dot Jones. You talk about special!

Dot Jones and her two sidekicks made the rounds of Colorado television and radio stations. They were everywhere. Meeting them with enough time to get acquainted was pure luck. Dot Jones, in case you don't recognize the name, has won the world championship in arm-wrestling for the past nine years. Nine years. Dot has never lost that championship. We talk not Denver or even U. S. here. This championship covers the entire world.

If someone had told me I might get to visit with the (women's) arm-wrestling champion I would have pictured some tough broad who swaggered around breaking people's arms and intimidating ordinary folks. I might have made up some cute phrase about the Mike Tyson of the corner bar, or some such. Wrong. Dot Jones is a really nice person. She's a juvenile officer in Fresno and cares intensely about her job and the kids she confronts in the line of duty. At six foot three and 245 pounds, she must make quite an impression on some kid about to help himself to a hubcap

One day later, speeding along I-25 north of Denver, a car pulled up alongside mine with frantic honking and waving. There sat Dot and her two "managers." Friendly as all get-out. She even opened her window to salute us with one of those massive arms. A gentle, caring human being, my new friend Dot.

That's the best thing about friends. They show up anywhere.

სა

# LAKESIDE REVISITED . . . WOW!

Straighten-up time has arrived here at my house, folks. Time for me to get the bills all paid, the car washed and serviced, the thank-you notes finished, and a supply of columns submitted to the newspapers well in advance. I need the decks cleared, in other words. Time has come for me to concentrate all of my attention and energies on shuffleboard.

Before I know it, I'll be on my way back to Lakeside, and this time I'd better know the rules.

Two years ago, when I first encountered Lakeside shufflers, nobody noticed whether or not I even understood the game. This year, big difference. Now my book, *Golden Roamers,* has been on the market for a few months, and shuffleboard counts with the characters in my story. I must know whereof I speak or I shall disgrace Bess and Ruth and Emmett and Lillian and the rest of those fictional people who became my friends during the course of writing the book. They posed as a shuffleboard club in order to disguise the fact that they'd stolen a Trailways bus.

My job as a novelist was to make that a believable story. That was accomplished only after some kindly Power sent me to Lakeside to make a speech about options and opportunities for those of us in our "third age," as the French refer to oldsters. Little did I imagine that I'd find any more at Lakeside than an audience. Since Lakeside, Ohio, is a Chautauqua institution, I counted on a good time and receptive listeners. But shuffleboard? I had no idea. I also had no idea how I was going to finish that book without more familiarity with shuffleboard. The entire project seemed doomed until I landed at Lakeside.

Families from all over the country congregate at Lakeside for a number of reasons but they all, of all ages, play shuffleboard. I watched, listened, made notes, had lessons, and generally submerged myself in shuffleboard during my stay. I enjoyed every minute. Not since Dad had a shuffleboard court painted on our front porch back in McPherson, Kansas, in the thirties had I played shuffleboard. Our approach to the game was casual, to say the least. Not at Lakeside.

Now — wonders of wonders — I have been invited to be at Lakeside, Ohio, for the Summer Nationals. I'll make a speech, talk about *Golden Roamers,* and have the best time I can imagine with those dedicated shufflers. What a delight that promises to be!

"Doesn't take much to get this woman worked up, does it?" You must be saying that to yourself about now. But let me tell you this:

When I started writing in my mid-fifties, all I intended to do was fill my time and find some sort of outlet for the energies that would keep me occupied enough to feel useful. I've had no aspirations or intentions to be rich or famous as a writer. But this recognition from Lakeside, Ohio, and from similar places because something I wrote struck a nerve — well, that beats any sort of response I ever envisioned for myself.

Sharing that elation with you, my readers, is important to me. So I'll study the rules and play the game — and love it.

❧

# WHY WE EAT WHAT WE EAT

Y ou should see the piles of books on my coffee table now!
Just a few weeks ago I had the whole mess cleared off. My
modest digs reflected, to my way of thinking, the new approach to
organization and neatness in my life. Then I started thinking and reading
more and more about the anthropology of food and went absolutely haywire
in a couple of bookstores ferreting out books about the eating history of the
world around us.

Plenty of people had delved into the fascination of foods long before I
emerged from my Milky Way world. In splendid bookstores, shelf after shelf
of books about food and society can be found right next to thousands of
cookbooks that prove the point.

Last fall, while in Italy with the Smithsonian, I heard lectures by an
anthropologist who introduced the idea of studying civilizations from the
standpoint of foodstuffs. He made it very clear that the availability of various
kinds of foods shaped the life styles of people all over the world. Of even
more fascination to me was his notion that the first separation of man from
the other forms of animal life began when men figured out how to provide,
prepare, and preserve food for future needs and wants.

The idea that you could have grain to grind and store without
wandering all over the western half of any continent must have been even
more of a boon to the budding housewife than was Bird's Eye frozen fish.
Cuisinart did not add nearly the excitement to our kitchens that those
primitive moms must have felt when they discovered the marvelous
improvement in the meat of a rabbit after dropping it in the fire for a while.

Life must have taken on new meaning because meat from one meal could be strung up and dried to be eaten later without going back out and chasing another enormous buffalo, which always wound up smelling so bad that you had to move the tents to get a good night's sleep.

Consider, too, the differences in food supplies in various parts of the world. Those aborigines in tropical climes had only to reach out and pluck a banana or a grape to get by, but the poor devils in the Antarctic had to wrestle themselves into a kayak and set out in search of a blubber supply. Some folks worked to eat, so they learned to work at everything else. The warmer-climate people tended to lie around waiting for a coconut to fall. Food supplies have shaped our cultures.

So what sort of books have I found? The first, *Why We Eat What We Eat* by Raymond Sokolov, points out the revolution in the food habits of this entire planet that resulted from Columbus's trip to this hemisphere. From that time on, the eating of the world changed because of the introduction of food from one half of the world to another. Cuisines changed more completely then than at any earlier time. Only the recent introduction of "nouvelle cuisine" compares with the metamorphosis of foodways beginning with Columbus. The banana-pluckers and the blubber-seekers combined talents, so to speak. It began with a search for spices.

Now at least twenty more books, from *The Appetite and the Eye* to *A History of Food: From Manna to Microwave,* await my study. You'll hear more about it.

෨

# AN AMERICAN INSTITUTION

From the minute I see the main gate I *feel* Chautauqua. Like smelling the chocolate before getting to Hershey. Like licking our fingers to taste the salt before crossing that last hill on the way to the beach. Anticipation! Those old butterflies in my middle react just as they used to on May Day back in Kansas sixty years ago. I just can't wait.

Often when these columns appear in your newspaper, my title has been replaced, usually by something better than I had written myself. I hope that doesn't happen with this one because I looked for a catchy title, hoping in my collection of materials about Chautauqua to find some descriptive phrase used by the institution. All I found: "An American Institution." What more would serve any real purpose?

Chautauqua, New York, has graced the shores of Lake Chautauqua, within throwing distance of Lake Erie on the most western edge of New York, since 1874. South from Buffalo about ninety minutes on I-90. Although we can find it on the maps, near Jamestown and Mayville, Chautauqua exists in a world of its own. That main gate leads to — as far as I'm concerned — a better way of life for all who enter. Three hundred ninety-one thousand of us do that every year during the nine-week season.

"What's with this woman?" you must be saying by now. "She's off her rocker raving about some place I've never even heard of!"

True, folks. Absolutely true. Although you have probably *have* heard of Chautauqua.

Early in this century the Chautauqua movement set out to enlighten all of America with traveling lectures and so on. Chautauqua still exists in

Boulder, Colorado, and Lakeside, Ohio. No advertising, no hype. Just a continuing emphasis on the quality of our lives.

A day or two ago I encountered a young man entering the post office here in Pueblo, Colorado. Nice looking guy, about the age of my sons. He took off his cap (that's important here) as he stopped to remark about how he likes these columns and my PBS series, "Midlife Musings." You can imagine how much I liked that!

Then he said, "I like it especially when you talk about values." Replaced his cap and was gone. I stood there staring after him. Values!

Therein lies my message about Chautauqua. Within the confines of that Victorian village those of us lucky enough to be there concentrate on values. The president of the Chautauqua Institution says, "Chautauqua with its artistic, intellectual, spiritual and recreational opportunities never leaves anyone unchanged." Creativity is encouraged among the narrow streets and wicker rockers on cottage porches.

But it's the values — the underlying principles of our lives — that we come in contact with in that tranquil place. No motor traffic, no loud noises, no sirens.

Conversation boils down to values there. Here's the big discovery: The desire to maintain our values of life style is not confined to such surroundings. Right here, right now, we can all pay attention to what's important in our lives.

Let's try.

෬

# WILL THE REAL CARY GRANT . . .

The name mentioned most often during games of Trivial Pursuit is Cary Grant. This is not a statistical revelation; it's my own observation.

Shakespeare and Arnold Palmer come close seconds, but Cary Grant is most memorable, most mentionable in the all-purpose and silver screen versions of the game, anyway. Among players of all ages, ahead of John Wayne, Gary Cooper, even Paul Newman or Robert Redford, Cary Grant is most guessed and precipitates the most conversations.

Perhaps I simply notice his name more often than other actors' because this is almost painful to me. I'd hate to be a name-dropping bore, but I do have a Cary Grant story. It's all I can do to keep from telling it ten times every evening. I bite my tongue a lot.

Cary Grant, his gorgeous young wife and I took a cruise together — the three of us and five or six hundred other passengers. Unlike many celebrity cruise guests, the Grants mingled with their fellow travelers and took an active part in shipboard life: singalongs around the piano and all that. They even played bingo and took dance lessons.

You should see him. Even in the morning he's Cary Grant. The accent, the manner, the tone of voice, the charm never slips. He was nearly eighty then — in 1983. His figure was trim, his posture perfect. He was not cutesy-smiley, just pleasant.

My kites interested him. I had several with me and collected more along the way from Hong Kong to Durban. One breezy day I was on the promenade deck at the stern of the ship messing with a Chinese kite. It was a silk phoenix bird that fluttered, soared, dipped and shuddered in the combination of crosswinds and hot air from the ship's engines.

I would launch the kite on the port side trying to keep it clear of railings, deck chairs and a few passengers. That feisty devil of a kite would dance around where I wanted him for a few minutes, dive dangerously close to the water, then invariably fly toward the center of the deck, flirting with the flagpole. For two hours or more I stayed there, totally absorbed in the air currents, the challenge of the unruly kite, the varying tugs on the line. I never let it out more than two hundred feet and had a marvelous time.

Once in a while I looked back toward the upper decks of the ship and noticed a couple leaning against the rail on the highest passenger deck. They waved at me, the stunning girl and the tanned, elegant man with snow-white hair and black-rimmed glasses. I waved back.

That evening, Cary Grant stopped at my table in the dining room. "You had a marvelous duel with that kite today. Barbara and I were fascinated watching you."

Now *that* has to be the Switch of the Century:

Cary Grant was watching *me!*

છ

# VI. TAKE IT FROM ME!

## ANY SMALL CHANGE WILL DO

Hey, what a great picture! Where in the world did you get that? Looks wonderful there above that table! New?" She peered through her bifocals, craning to see a recognizable signature. This friend peeks at the bottoms of my plates, too. "Who's the artist?"

This woman made those remarks in my own living room, which certainly pleased me. I had to admit the painting she so admired had been hanging in the hallway around the corner for nigh unto six years. She'd simply missed it. But moving that picture no more than fifteen feet made a difference, brightening my living room and my life.

After she left (finally!), the thought remained. Moving that one painting had made a difference. Mostly, I suppose, because it hangs opposite the chair in which I usually sit. My outlook had brightened since my "landscape" had been altered. The moved-out wood-cut gave the hallway a boost, too.

Then the adrenaline started to flow. I grabbed the Robert Rivera gourd-pot from its place of honor on the dining room table. It had sat there since a trip to Santa Fe four years ago. In its place, a basket of apples. Wow! Did that ever look bright and welcoming for anyone coming through the front door!

Images of what to put there next already crowded my head. A fall arrangement of squash, eggplant, chilies, or corn? Beets? I was on a roll here, feeling fine about disrupting the status quo of my surroundings. Who can complain about boredom when we have all our stuff to move around without even shoving the couch to the other wall or calling in a decorator?

Two lessons here, as far as I can see: We can apply the same treatment for house-bound oldsters who despair of the sameness of their day-to-day lives. By the same token, our lives, not just our living rooms, can be made more stimulating, more interesting to us and to others, by making a few small changes one at a time. Whether we hang something different over the mantel, around our necks, or on our calendar, we can shift focus.

Back to that first "lesson:" Before our mother needed full-time care of a nursing facility she sat in the same chair surrounded by the same stuff every day. The sameness took its toll. She was listless and bored most of the time. One day my sister and I insisted on switching paintings. First she objected, which at least improved her circulation momentarily. Then she approved and thanked us for the improvement. We knew we could not cure all of her ills but any change of scene helps — particularly since there's no way to convince these really old people to sit in some other chair to get another view of their world.

Now that she is in the nursing home we can still switch the family pictures on the wall where she can look at a variety of faces from her bed. Double value. She remembers more of the family and we think we've done something for Mother.

So who's bored? Try taking a look at the sameness in your own life. How "set-in-your-ways" are you? Could it possibly be you bore yourself?

If so, just move it. That's all.

⁀

# HOW OLD WAS YOUR BROTHER?

Lately I've been on a storytelling jag. I find myself hunting for cassettes of storytellers to carry in the car for long drives. I look at books I might want to read, assessing their value as a source of storytelling material. Down in Taos, New Mexico, the storyteller dolls attracted my attention, although some of those for sale are pathetic reproductions of the original charmers. Still, storytelling comes through as a means of communicating on a different level.

Telling a story can be more than entertainment. We all recognize the value of telling our children the lessons of life through stories about what happened to little girls who didn't eat the crusts of their bread. Their hair didn't curl, wasn't that it? We told our sons in lurid detail about what had happened to other little boys who dawdled on the way home from school. Lying? Oh, no. We told stories to make a point. Kids are more apt to listen to stories than to reason.

The stories of Garrison Keillor or the Adirondack storytellers are much more interesting and certainly more imaginative than are the ones we used to make a point about cleaning your plate. Yet even those tales carry an underlying way of saying in a roundabout manner something that might ruin somebody's day if you blurted it right out.

There's an example of such a story in my husband's family. Most of us shy away from talking about dying, particularly as that subject applies directly to us. Fear of the unknown has a lot to do with it. Once in a while, however, the topic does come up. Folks back in Concordia, Kansas, had a pragmatic attitude.

Joe Weaver worked in the post office. Day in and day out, most of the townspeople appeared at Joe's window, generally with time to visit. One morning many years ago the conversation went like this:

"Morning, Joe. Say, I'm sorry to hear about your brother Ross dyin'."

"Thanks, Bert."

"How old was Ross, Joe?"

"Brother Ross was fifty-six, Bert."

"How 'bout your brother Glenn, Joe?"

"Glenn died a couple years ago, Bert."

"How old was Glenn when he went, Joe?"

"Glenn was fifty-two, Bert."

"And how about your dad, Joe?"

"Oh, Dad was a doctor, Bert, like my brothers."

"No, Joe. I mean how old was he when he died?"

"My dad was fifty-eight when he died, Bert."

"Oh. How old are you now, Joe?"

"I just turned fifty-five, Bert."

Bert laughed so hard his face turned crimson and he nearly choked. He slapped his knee and sputtered.

"Don't seem like it would pay you to buy a suit of clothes with two pairs of pants, does it, Joe?"

❧

# BARBARA, THE BURNING BUSH

**B**oy, am I proud of her! Barbara Bush doesn't know it yet, but her commencement speech to the graduating class at Wellesley College sent chills up my spine, brought tears to my eyes and hope to my troubled spirit.

Most of us have recognized our First Lady as a woman living by traditional standards. Her value system has to be a lot like mine — her evaluation of herself and her role as a woman and mother, I mean. What I failed to appreciate earlier was made perfectly clear from that speakers' platform in Massachusetts. At long last the women of my age — women who grew up believing we have a special niche to fill, a preordained role to play that is our own — women like me have the finest, most articulate spokesman we have had in years.

And there are millions of us.

Quotations from that speech will endure long after the anchormen and the other media persons so astonished by this remarkable woman's presence have gone on to other jobs. Long after George Bush has left the White House, Barbara's poise, grace, considerate manner, and determination will be recognized as a definitive statement of the importance of family life and personal relationships in the American scheme of things.

"The future of America does not depend on what goes on in the White House. It depends on what happens in your house."

Mrs. Bush's reference to old age was poignant and equally well-stated. Approximate quote: "At the end of your life, you will never regret not having passed one more test, not winning one more verdict or not closing one more deal. You will regret time not spent with a husband, a child, a friend, or a parent." Bless you, lady.

One of her most telling remarks: "It's not baby-sitting when it's your kids."

Of course, we sixty-five-year-old girls have seen First Ladies come and go. The most we recall of them hangs on mannequins at the Smithsonian. Thinking back about First Ladies I Have Lived Through, I can't say much about Mrs. Coolidge. Neither did Mr. Coolidge. Mrs. Hoover sometimes wore a Girl Scout uniform, as I recall. Eleanor Roosevelt was a brilliant, forward-looking woman, but her voice was nasal and raspy, her speeches genuinely dull, and her manner often one of condescension.

Bess Truman might rank closest to my current heroine in terms of down-to-earth humanity. Mamie was forever a commanding officer's wife. Pat Nixon added nothing to the national scene and Jackie Baby looked better than she sounded. Lady Bird was all business, Rosalynn all Southern Charm. Betty Ford needed mostly to care for herself and displayed greater strength after her White House years. Nancy Reagan acted as if she thought she was playing the mean lead in a soap. Then here comes Barbara — straight-forward, proud, generous — and shooting from the hip.

God bless you, First Lady, for choosing to devote your life and your talents to your husband, home and family, to those human relationships you stressed in that speech. Thanks for speaking up for the rest of us.

☙

# BLAME THIS WHOLE MESS ON DR. SPOCK!

A s far as I'm concerned, we can blame the whole mess on Dr. Spock. That's right, Dr. Benjamin Spock. And it won't hurt my feelings if you tell him I said so.

Criticizing that leading authority on child-rearing is tantamount to casting doubts on the sincerity of Albert Schweitzer or Mother Theresa. You might as well question Roger Tory Peterson's identification of a bird or Jacques Cousteau's interpretation of the antics of sea anemones in times of stress, I'll admit that.

But please think about this for the two minutes or so it'll take you to read this column.

About the time John and I got into the child-raising business, Dr. Spock decided that no child should *have* to do anything. No more would any mini-ego be damaged by unwanted carrots or instructions to leave other kids' toys alone. "Permissive" became the byword. "Self-expression" was the key to ultimate happiness.

No more should some tyke be expected to keep his room neat or color within the lines. Our first-born insisted upon playing with her strained spinach, messing it all over the tray of the high chair, onto the rug, into my hair. The Book suggested that the child needed more of a creative outlet — finger paints. Dutifully, we supplied the finger paints before feeding the budding genius. She ate the paints, wet paper and all, then messed around with the baby food anyway.

Dr. Spock faded in importance at our house about that time. But the neighbor's unleashed brats could wander in and out of my house, uninvited and unannounced, wreaking havoc as they passed. Whenever I heard a tiny voice piping, "Here comes Kevin!" trouble was brewing.

But Kevin's mother smiled serenely. Kevin was free to express himself. Kevin was free to bust up the Weaver kids' stuff. Kevin was reasoned with about putting on his boots even when there was snow up to his ears and the school bus was waiting.

Liberating do-gooders adopted the same philosophies in schools. No need to badger the little darlings into finishing an assignment or taking silly tests; they would learn at their own rate. Each child could do as he pleased. Days of sitting still in your desk and, by George, learning to spell and read and write legibly gave way to fitting round pegs into square holes and to personality testing. Modern methods. Students smoked on the school grounds and made fun of anyone who made straight "A"s.

What does this have to do with today's world? Plenty, I say.

Not long ago, Dr. Spock was interviewed on the fiftieth anniversary of his book, or fiftieth printing, or some such. Loudly he bemoaned the state of the American family. Too much divorce, appalling statistics about child neglect and other crimes. "Married couples today just don't try," he pontificated.

Now wait a minute, there, Doc. Parents of today's couples let them grow up thinking that the greatest goal in life was self-satisfaction.

Divorce? Drugs? They were raised by your book, Doc!

They're still living by it, Doc.

So are their kids, Doc.

છ૭

# PHOTOS

My days as an enthusiastic photographer are numbered — not only by the two small albums of presentable pictures on my coffee table, but even more by the hundreds of yellow envelopes filled with rotten snapshots that are crowding me out of my closets. I am about to be inundated by unidentified, undated landscapes and the faces of smiling strangers.

I have unlabeled pictures of: long-forgotten Christmas pageants. A boy riding a headless, legless horse. Look-alike newborn babies, sleeping. People apparently flying kites. The back of my mother's head. My emu — sitting down. The Governor's National Oyster Shucking Championship trophy presented by St. Mary's Rotary Club, wherever that might be. A starfish on a rock in front of somebody's bare feet. Antebellum mansions. Unrecognizable specks purported to be seals in Glacier Bay.

All of these and more lurk in shoe boxes and grocery sacks; an ever growing tidal wave of Kodak paper and Polaroid prints. Naturally, I have saved the negatives in case I need reprints.

The time has come to put this treasure-trove to good use. First of all, I am going to include a snapshot with everything I mail in an envelope. Not just letters, although it is sure to be intensely interesting to my friends when I send a picture of two dogs with my thank-you notes. When I pay my bills, I intend to favor my creditors with a photo of Squirrel Creek or the Taos Pueblo. My Christmas card list will have to be expanded enormously to get rid of these murky views of Chesapeake Bay and the Great Wall. I cannot simply throw them away.

Best of all, I'll have some more enlargements made. That's the most fun. I recommend it to all of my friends who share this problem: Have some five-by-sevens made of your worst pictures, then show them to your guests with a straight face when the party seems to sag. They'll say insipid things like, "Oh, how nice. Is that a waterfall?" or, "That baby looks just like your side of the family."

Titles add to the enjoyment of this game. My best are entitled "Two Cars and a Bush," "Man Feeding a Fish to a Bird," and "Asphalt in Portugal."

One word of warning: Do not decide to search through the boxes of yellow envelopes for material for a newspaper column.

You'll waste the whole day.

❧

## PRESS 1 FOR WHAT?

Years ago I wrote one of my first columns about the difficulties I experienced in getting telephone service when first establishing residence in upstate New York. Certainly I can't expect you to recall that episode of my life as a fifty-eight-year-old freshman in college.

The woman at the desk in the Nynex office instructed me to go to the telephone across the room to call her up to place my request. We talked to each other by phone while watching each other across an uncrowded room. The frustration was palpable. I would have settled for two tin cans and a piece of string.

That happened eleven years ago. In my estimation, phone service has gone downhill ever since, in the name of progress.

One of my sisters endured the hardship of moving telephone service in Arizona. She didn't even have the part about calling the woman in the office. By now the entire civilized world lives by "Press 1 now if you want . . ."

Although Mary was curious about what might be reached by pressing some other number, the urgency of the recorded voice had her pushing that "1" button so fast it made your head swim. The next voice told her to press some other number for who-knows-what. By the time she had completely followed the instruction coming out of that great U S West in the wild blue yonder, Mary heard only a busy signal and instructions to try again later.

Never once did a real voice come on the line. Never once could she contact a real person who could respond to her requests.

Finally, after literally days of trying to accomplish what should amount to a simple task in today's electronic world, the phone arrangements were screwed up anyway. Wrong day. My poor little sister, not even old enough for Medicare yet, stood helplessly in the middle of moving boxes, cartons and mattresses, waving a dead telephone instrument above her head. "This is my umbilical cord! Our lives depend on this thing!" she shouted. I ducked, trying not to step on her dog cowering in the corner.

Matters became even more complex when Mary tried to call her bank concerning transfers of funds with closing of sales and all the rigmarole of any real-estate transaction. What did she get? "Press 1." The entire banking network has only one number — impossible to call the nice young man in the branch you patronize. Recorded, maybe synthesized, voices instruct the caller to punch this or that until at last a human answers, telling you you have the wrong number.

At times like these, those good old days do look good, don't they? Al Jolson sang, "Hello, Central, give me heaven 'way down in Tennessee." I miss Central. What's more, Central probably misses her job.

That's one thing I cannot figure out: On one hand we are devastated by unemployment while on the other we are destroying personal jobs and service as fast as we can.

Remember the book *Future Shock?* We were warned about this happening. Automation not only has wiped out jobs, it has obliterated much of our sense of communication with a real world.

I'd call someone to complain, but I don't know which number to press.

&

# WHAT WAS THE TAX ON MINE?

L isten up, ladies! We absolutely *must* do something about the way we handle the bill when we eat out in a group! Until we resolve that problem, we can never claim true equality.

Have you ever seen six men at a table in a restaurant saying, "Now, Sam had the crab salad, and that was a dollar more than my turkey sandwich"? Have you watched the glances become glares as waiters stand around waiting for us to find out if decaf costs the same as regular coffee? Separate checks are out of the question in any place ritzier than fast-food chains, any more. We women are going to have to cope with the situation.

Until eight of us had dinner in a classy French restaurant in Boston, I was convinced that women traveling alone can handle any problem. My faith was shaken that night. Three of us had no cocktails, although I had mineral water, which costs much less than a martini, of course. The price spread of the entrees on the menu was ten dollars. Salad was extra. So was soup. Not everyone had dessert, but we all enjoyed watching the waiter's expertise in preparing crepes suzette for two.

When the check came, amounting to just a little less than the national debt, only one of our party knew the price of her dinner. She had chicken.

I'd chosen the restaurant. I could jolly well handle the finances. Without delay. The waiter patiently brought the menus back and the recital began of who had what and how much was fifteen per cent of that? Charging the whole mess on a card and leaving with some semblance of aplomb would have made matters worse — trying to split up the total depended on menu prices, and the menus were much too fancy to take with us.

Bills of all denominations landed in front of me with remarks like, "That should cover mine," but were shuffled in with other stacks of money. Eventually, we had rounded up more than necessary — fifteen per cent is fifteen per cent, and we were not going to be gauche enough to over-tip so we started handing one-dollar bills back around the table, laughing like schoolgirls at the fair.

Believe me, the next time I have dinner out with a bunch of women, I will have a notebook and pencil at the ready. I will pass the notebook around the table as each person orders, asking her to record her name and the price of her meal. If necessary, I'll send it around again when dessert and coffee are ordered, or even the second glass of wine. Quietly. Then when I have to function as Troop Treasurer, I'll be ready, and so will my friends.

I hope I don't forget that. It's not a bad idea.

∽

# WHAT'S SO FUNNY ABOUT THAT?

Once in a while, someone attempts to analyze humor. In almost any crowd, particularly among those who know a little bit about a lot of things, some self-proclaimed clown will pontificate about what makes people laugh. They believe you can anatomize humor. (I found that word "anatomize" when I needed to know if analyze is spelled with an *s* or a *z*. Either can be used for analyse/ze. Anatomize means "dissect." So . . .)

In my trusty *Oxford Concise Dictionary* I found that humor or "comicality" means "less intellectual and more sympathetic than wit." That doesn't help much, does it?

Plunging ever further into my own research on the subject — mostly because I feel the world seems a mite short of laughability these days — I chose to concentrate on Dave Barry's work. On the cover of Dave Barry's *Greatest Hits* the *New York Times* book review is quoted: "Mr. Barry is the funniest man in America and we should encourage him. Buy this book."

Somehow I get the feeling Mr. Barry came up with that blurb himself. Book reviewers generally lack that much of a sense of humor.

Dave Barry has won the Pulitzer Prize for being so darned funny. He had his picture taken for the cover illustration of this Fawcett-published book sitting in what appears to be the Hudson River with his personal computer keyboard in his lap and his bare feet sticking out. He's wearing a striped necktie and a worried look. Well, he has a suit on, too. Navy blue. The computer cord can be seen sticking out of the water. There's mud on the keyboard. Maybe that means that's the East River.

At any rate, with eleven books out ahead of this one (1988), Mr. Barry certainly knows what funny means. I know he's funny because I laugh myself to sleep happily taking small doses of Barry:

"What bothers me about yuppies is, they're destroying the normal social order, which is that people are supposed to start out as wild-eyed radicals, and then gradually, over time, develop gum disease and become conservatives."

The anatomizers would tell us that the unexpected but appropriate reference to gum disease makes this statement hilarious. Barry continues with a plan for his readers (we who no longer laugh at the concept of hemorrhoids) to cope with yuppies. Quiet but amusing, and carrying a real grain of truth about our world as he sees it.

Dave Barry has experienced many of our own life-shaping events. We relate to his stories. That must be one of the secrets. Take his account of the nativity pageant from his youth in Armonk, New York:

"Many were the happy rehearsal hours we shepherds spent back there in the dark, whacking each other with sticks and climbing up the ladder . . ."

Parenting a young son provides material for Dave's columns, too. He recounts what happened the day his four-year-old son heard him use a word forbidden for family usage.

Said the kid: "Daddy, you shouldn't say the s-word."

Reports the father: "He was merely trying to correct my behavior . . . but I got a condescending lecture from a person who consistently puts his underpants on backwards."

I say that's humor. You figure out why.

&

## WHICH SIDE WOULD YOU HAVE CHOSEN?

Remember choosing sides? Back in Kansas, in grade school, nothing could rival choosing up sides for importance in our days. Whether the sides competed in a spelling bee, work-up baseball at recess, or dodge-ball in gym, standing there waiting for one of the captains to pick out their spellers or players turned our insides to mush. We not only wanted to be on the winning team, we prayed to be chosen quickly.

Growing older, I began to think of choosing sides in the opposite direction. Which team would I have wanted to join, faced with some crucial decisions? Particularly reading history, I often wondered: "Which side would I have been on in *that* war?" "How would I have voted on *that* issue?" Or, "Would I have marched in *that* parade?"

In the first place, I know I would never have settled the New World. Those people had more pure nerve than I can ever imagine in myself. The mountain men and the early explorers make our astronauts look tame. Granted, they didn't head for the moon, but they had no contact with the world they left behind and no real idea what they faced.

No way can I picture myself trudging along behind a Conestoga wagon, tearing my skirts on tumbleweed and cactus, smiling bravely when the water holes turned out to be dried up and the oxen died. No matter what century, my life style would never have encompassed cooking over an open fire waiting for dad and the boys to bring in the beaver pelts.

If some handsome devil had talked me into going out there, would I have been concerned about saving the buffalo about to stampede over my sod house? Would Twentieth Century specialists in hindsight accuse my family and me of wanton destruction because we tried to grow wheat, or would I have been the only one in the crowd trying to preserve the prairies? Would I have invited folks who looked like savages over for supper and offered to teach their squaws to knit? No. I would have stayed at home in Boston where I belonged.

The physical challenges and tribulations still don't bother me as much as do the moral issues our ancestors have faced, the decisions they have suffered through, the "rights" for which they have died.

Some perfectly honest, good folks must have been on the other side of what we now see as cut-and-dried right and wrong. Some of our forefathers might have been loyal to King George and felt they were absolutely justified in that position. How many thousands died for the Confederacy, positive their view of their world was the right one? We oversimplify on the side of the winners. Or magnify the plight of "victims" to suit our point of view.

So why should I take your time and mine to ponder such questions now? Well, it seems to me we are in yet another time of major change and we'll be forced to choose sides. The world has been pretty well filled up, so we needn't worry about risking our lives on new frontiers. Civil rights and equal opportunities have a long way to go, but we understand the goals and the purposes now.

It's the changing aspects of morality, of sexual practice, that I must now evaluate and choose my side. So must you. And we can't wait for history books to tell us which side wins.

☙

## OH, HOW WE DANCED!

W hat should I do about my mother's wedding anniversary?" The man calling the talk show psychologist on KOA in Denver cared about his question.

"My dad died about six months ago, and next month will be their fiftieth anniversary. I know she had been counting on a big party for years. What can I do to help my mother through this trying time?"

Expert advice met with my approval. Write a nice, not sticky, note about how much Mother means to you and how you have been thinking of her in the approach of this anniversary. Give her some sort of a present, but not the typical anniversary gift. After all, this woman has devoted a half century to keeping this family going just as much as did her husband. At least, we can assume that. She deserves recognition, even if she's single now.

The worst way to treat a widow on the anniversary of her marriage, particularly one that lasted at least his lifetime, is silence. Often we hesitate because we don't know what to say, or we fear blurting out the wrong words. Just a simple "This day has special meaning for you. How about lunch?" will ease a friend over the reminders that can make for a dismal day. Once you've said that much, indulge in only as much "good-old-days" talk as the widow initiates.

Good old days have been spinning in this head, too. That man with his question triggered a real response in me because of an impending anniversary of my own. This will be the thirteenth time that date has rolled around since John died after thirty-four years of marriage.

Do you realize that's more than twelve thousand days? No wonder we miss the old boys! Break that down into football seasons, camping trips, Cub Scout meetings, visits to grandparents, Christmas Eve services, lawn-mowing, garage-cleaning, fireworks, Sunday night suppers, swim meets, country-club dances, medical conventions, income-tax estimates, and trips to the Safeway. We're talking major involvement, here.

Most families remember to mention the anniversary date. Mine have always been very good about that: July 3, 1945. After so long a time the recollection of long-ago wedding days becomes more than nostalgia. Looking back at wartime marriage can be downright funny.

John was in the Army. I had just graduated from college. Shortages dictated what we wore and where we could go. Rayon dresses. Leg makeup. Short honeymoon on Dad's "C" card for rationed gas. Crowded trains. Stamps for butter and cheese and meat. Our first home consisted of two rooms with an icebox that flooded the kitchen daily because I never remembered to empty the pan underneath.

Now forty-seven years have passed. The family and I have survived. We've grown in ways that would have been a credit to our "head of the household."

This year I'm getting myself a present. I've decided to buy a really nice frame for my favorite picture from our wedding book. We both look so young, so eager, so full of our new life together.

That might be a good gift idea for that man who called KOA.

&

# TALENTED KIDS, L. A. STYLE

Have you just about given up on today's youngsters? Do you and your neighbors gather at the supermarket and bemoan the degradation of our kids and grandkids — the way they dress, the "music" they enjoy, the way they drive? Have you despaired of our country's future because the youngsters you see never comb their hair or hold the door for old ladies? Last week I would have agreed with you. The U. S. A. must be headed for hell in a hand basket!

As a matter of strict fact, I think my grandmother felt the same way about our generation back in the days of Benny Goodman and *Flat Foot Floogie*. I wish Grandmother were still around so I could tell her about the kids I saw in Los Angeles. Old Gram would have loved this.

Colors United entertained one evening during a convention of the California Association of Hospitals and Health Services, an organization made up of volunteers. If you watched the Super Bowl, you saw Colors United perform during half-time with Michael Jackson. Quite a show. Hundreds of young people all singing and carrying on in the name of brotherhood and the good life. We at this meeting saw only a small part of that crowd, but we saw enough to recall these kids with wonder for years to come.

Colors United members are students at Watts High School in Los Angeles. With the inspired leadership of two or three adults, these kids have emerged from their tawdry world of gangs, drugs, booze, and violence to find a new and better way to live.

After their electrifying presentation of music, dancing, and good-humored horseplay, they answered questions from the audience about their backgrounds and their future. Kids rising above their own expectations and their own predicament thrilled that crowd.

Another very different. yet quite the same, thrill came the next day. The general meeting opened with an explosive entrance into the meeting hall (actually two ballrooms of the Hilton Universal City) by members of the marching band of the University of Southern California. In the splendid shining brass Trojan helmets and red and gold capes, tooting tubas and beating drums, those kids created a different kind of a stir among those folks.

Bursting through the doors and down the aisles of the meeting room, that band had the twelve hundred people gathered there transfixed with the glorious joy of a Sousa march. Then they played and we sang the National Anthem. Most of us cried.

The fight song of USC, so familiar, brought some back on their feet. Rousing, that's what it was, rousing! The thirty-piece band finished off with a roof-shaking rendition of *Sing Sing Sing* from the Benny Goodman days and we shouted in joy. Exhilarating beyond belief.

All kids. All musicians. All working their way into their own futures from very different backgrounds. The contrasts and the similarities of two groups of performers have seldom been so graphically demonstrated before my eyes.

What did they have in common besides the music and the audience? Looking into their eyes, sharing their enthusiasm, it struck me:

What these so-different kids share is a solid sense of belonging. We were blessed by their presence.

ॐ

## "WILT THOU TAKE THIS . . ."

I'm preparing a questionnaire for selecting my second wife. Any woman who wants to marry me will have to fill out an application." A pompous little man actually said that to me. He even explained his method of screening applicants through his attorney's office. Something about a blind ad in only the best newspapers.

I thought he was joking at first, but this jerk was serious. He even told me the first two questions: "How much money do you have?" and "Do you get seasick?" You can imagine the rest of the quiz. Any woman desperate enough to fill in the blanks was also required to submit a complete medical record. Mr. Important, of course, had no intention of discussing his finances, politics, or previous sex life with the applicants. There would be no mention of his arthritis.

In spite of my disgust with his chauvinist attitude, I was forced to agree there is a need for older people contemplating marriage to settle some arguments before they start establishing compatibility. After all, they won't have the first fifteen or twenty years to work out the kinks in their relationship like young marrieds can.

"Second marriage is the triumph of optimism over experience," I have read. That's not necessarily so, but after thirty-four years of the first go-round, deliver me from any man who refuses to dance and/or play bridge — at least once in a while.

Retired couples, with so much togetherness, should have similar tastes in food, travel, and general interests. Congenial attitudes about money are essential, too.

I wish now I had prepared a list of really important questions for that egomaniac:

Do you like casseroles? Brunches? Do you consider eating out a last resort? Is a fishing trip more important to you than a nice weekend at a fine hotel?

Do you object to pantyhose left overnight on the towel rack? Have you ever folded sheets? What do you feed your dog? Where does he sleep? Will you eat leftovers? Omelets? Chinese food? Lime Jello?

Did your first wife bake cookies? Make pasta? Iron? Do you display family pictures in the living room? Is your mother still living? Near here? Do you watch *Masterpiece Theater*? *Let's Make a Deal*?

Do you believe in rigid household budgets? Balancing bank statements to the penny? Are you tolerant of occasional small overdrafts? How long do you keep newspapers? Magazines? Letters? Do you like long walks? Glenn Miller? Museums?

Perhaps I'll settle for a questionnaire for gigolos. That would be much simpler — only a couple of questions.

જી

## WHERE IS HE, THE MAN WITH THE STAR?

One of these days — one of these days! — someone with much more clout than I'll ever have is going to recognize what's missing: Service.

That's what's so hard to find. Service is no more than a demonstration of what we think of each other as fellow human beings, and it's certainly on the endangered list, if not extinct.

Driving around Colorado hunting for that blessed sign FULL SERVICE at a so-called service station brought this problem to mind again. I worry about it a lot. Pumping gas is not my forté. I'm not on that committee. Most women my age, and there are more of us every day, have a hard time being ladylike while wrestling with an unruly stiff hose, a gas-tank cap that refuses to let go, and a nozzle that squirts gas all over our shoes before we can ram it into the car because of that wretched little flap in the way.

We need not return to the horse and buggy, but it would be thoughtful if someone would pay some attention to the needs and wants of the fastest-growing segment of the population — the good old girls. A few cents saved on a gallon of gas cannot compare with the satisfaction of having a clean windshield and knowing the oil is O.K. Far more tempting than a convenience store filled with a complete assortment of Pepperidge Farm cookies is a caring person asking to check the fluid in my transmission.

I'm having some awards printed up that I intend to carry with me at all times. Tasteful cards, maybe even a ribbon or gold seal attached, which will say something like, "Weaver Award for Thoughtful Service." I might even have a special gold-edged "Clean Restroom" version, just in case I run into an establishment where someone has taken time out from the computer at the front window long enough to tidy things up a bit.

Remember those lively, virile, attractive men who used to sing on Milton Berle's show? "We're the men from Texaco, we work from Maine to Mexico!" Or, "You can trust your car to the man who wears the star?" They're as hard to find these days as a real flying horse at a Mobil station or a tiger leaping out of anyone's gas tank. One surly individual to read the computers and write up the credit cards and sell maps and Milky Ways is the entire sales/service force. God help you if your engine sounds funny or the dome lights won't go off.

This old woman is nuts, you're saying. The world has changed, but some of us are still trying. Right. Close to home, some of us have a reliable old friend at the gas station. My old buddy, Bud Lee in Pueblo, knows my car like the back of his hand and he offers smiling service. Same for my regular stop at Lake George.

Out on the road is the problem. Loading up the car with a friend or two and taking off for several days is a great outing for women in our sixties — but not when we have to wrestle gas pumps.

One of these days!

ℰℛ

## TIME OUT — FOR WHAT?

U p in Minnesota about State Fair time, everyone gets excited about the lumberjack contest. No wonder. Paul Bunyan and his blue ox enjoy hero status in Minnesota.

I heard a tale about a legendary Minnesota lumberjack they called Olaf. That figures. Olaf weighed in around 230 pounds, stood well over six feet tall, and was reputed to be even stronger than Paul Bunyan. Each year for twenty years Olaf entered the lumberjack contest at the state fair and he won consistently. Others tried to chop the contest logs in two, but Olaf beat them hands down. Without so much as mopping his brow, Olaf whacked his way through to victory year after year.

On his twenty-first entry into the annual contest Olaf faced a new challenger, Bob. Bob impressed the crowd before the contest began. Beside Bob, Olaf seemed to have shrunk over the years. Bob stood taller. The muscles in his bulging forearms made the young girls in the crowd gasp. Bob looked like a lineman with the Dallas Cowboys. Olaf stared and so did everybody else.

"Looks like Old Olaf has had it this time," the astonished youngsters in the audience whispered to each other. They had never dared to call him "Old Olaf" before.

While Bob flexed his biceps and took a few practice swings, Olaf stood stock still. Even his mother was heard to remark something about Olaf "getting a little thick around the middle." A few side bets encouraged Bob enough that he swung his ax in wide arcs around his head just to show off.

As soon as the signal was given, both men tore into those logs with a vengeance. They chopped mightily, Bob's swings noticeably higher and louder than Olaf's. After about ten minutes, Olaf stopped whacking, looked around, and walked off the platform. The crowd stared in silence. Had Olaf conceded defeat? Oh, no. Back came Olaf to chop some more, but Bob never slackened his pace. If anything, he chopped faster.

Twice more Olaf pulled the same stunt — walked off and returned. This third time he resumed swinging the ax at the log and in no time at all he had won the contest. The crowd waved and cheered as if Olaf had been their choice all along. Olaf smiled and accepted the trophy for the twenty-first time.

Bob strode across the platform, hand extended to congratulate Olaf, but before he shook hands with the older man he asked one question.

"You won fair and square, Olaf, you're a good man. But what were you doing those times you walked off and came back?"

Olaf shrugged. "Sharpening my ax."

This week I'm doing what Olaf did: sharpening my ax. At Elderhostel, ax-sharpening could be called the order of the day. Interesting, alert people from all over the country have converged on Apache Junction, Arizona, for a week of study of Indian culture, western literature, and the life of the Sonoran Desert.

I'll admit I'd never have thought of Apache Junction as a wellspring of learning, but that all changed with the advent of Elderhostel.

Brace yourselves, folks. My ax is really sharp now.

❧

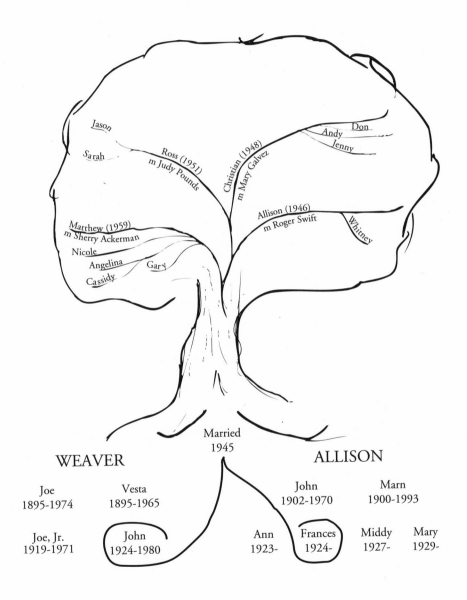

Jason

Sarah

Ross (1951)
m Judy Pounds

Christian (1948)
m Mary Galvez

Don
Andy
Jenny

Matthew (1959)
m Sherry Ackerman

Nicole

Angelina    Gary

Cassidy

Allison (1946)
m Roger Swift

Whitney

Married
1945

WEAVER                                      ALLISON

Joe              Vesta                John              Marn
1895-1974        1895-1965            1902-1970         1900-1993

Joe, Jr.         John                 Ann     Frances   Middy     Mary
1919-1971        1924-1980            1923-   1924-      1927-     1929-

# A TOUCH OF IMMORTALITY

D id you ever play "punch the icebox?" How about "kick the can?"
Did you ever sit on somebody's porch steps drinking
lemonade made of hand-squeezed lemons, wolfing down warm
popcorn while you waited for the lightning bugs to come out? Sixty years
ago — and more — I took part in those great games, savored that lemonade,
and collected blinking bugs in empty mayonnaise jars. I did it all again last
week. Home again in Kansas, I indulged in the ultimate nostalgia: a drive
down Walnut Street just after dark on a warm spring evening.

Great writers and deep thinkers tell us we can't go home again.
Certainly they are right about curbing our expectations and giving up the
notion we'll find that world as we left it. But appreciating our roots, our
background? Hey, in a little town, resurrecting the sights and smells, the
sense of living right there, comes easily.

But it's better if you discover this alone, after dark, when the dogs are in
and the folks are watching TV.

Right in front of "our house" (how many years ago?) I parked the rental
car and began my stroll. First I had to walk around the yard on the retaining
wall, then crossed the street to Grandmother's. In that moment, yesterday
began. The old elm trees we leaned against to hide our eyes when we were
"it" are gone, now. Cracks in the sidewalk have been patched again — and
again.

But the voices were there, echoing down Walnut Street. I "heard"
running footsteps as the rest of the kids scattered to hide while I counted to a
hundred because I couldn't guess who punched me on the back. They had

ganged behind me, shouting "Draw a circle, draw a square, take a finger and punch right *there!*"

Standing on the corner, I could hear them. Good thing nobody came along on this trip, I thought. Had my sisters been along, they would have had a better idea about where to hide and all that. Had my family been along, they would have had me confined for observation. Some of the old playmates might have gone along with the illusion, perhaps, but they all go to bed so early these days they can't come out to play.

Confirmation of the joys and privilege of growing up in such a place as McPherson, Kansas, hit a new high the next morning when I called on Miss Reichardt. If someone had walked into the fourth grade at Roosevelt School in 1933 (after knocking, of course) and announced to the class hunched over our desks practicing penmanship, "In sixty years you will come back to visit with Miss Reichardt," we would have decided the guy belonged with Buck Rogers. Miss Reichardt was the teacher. So she was already old.

"Of course, Frances. Do come over. I'll be at home this morning." She said that. I thought I might faint. A favorite teacher, push-pulls and all. Her house is neat and trim and so is Miss Reichardt. She stands erect, thinks straight, and lives in today's world. We discussed my grandchildren.

She's a McPherson Person.

I told her that being a good teacher is as close as most people can come to immortality. I believe that. I walked away with tears in my eyes and with small voices echoing on her street, too.

&#x2766;

# REMEMBER THE FAT GUY?

Who was that big fat guy? The one without a name tag?"

"Beats me! He sure seemed to remember me, but I didn't recognize him. I thought you'd know."

"He grabbed my hand like we were long-lost buddies. Was he that fat when we were in school?"

"Well, I can't think of his name for the life of me. I'll go ask my wife. Maybe she'll . . ."

I listened to that conversation without a word because I knew who the fat guy was. He was my husband, doing what he liked best: attending other people's class reunions. He loved to walk into a room filled with self-conscious, often pompous "boys of the old school" — all intent upon looking prosperous, young, and fashionably undernourished — all wearing name tags.

The routine was inevitable. John (my husband the surgeon) called everyone by name (tag). The opening gambit was something like, "Sam! You haven't changed a bit! Looks like the world's treating you just fine!"

To the women he always remarked, "You're even prettier than you were in school!"

The replies were equally fatuous. Everyone pretended to know him. They asked about his business and whether or not he had any grandchildren. His answers varied. He left a wake of startled faces, all whispering to each other, "Who *was* that fat guy?"

Such harmless intrusions whenever we happened to find a reunion in progress were far more entertaining than were any of our own reunions. We would have had to be slim and successful like the rest of our crowd there. We tried one medical-school reunion in Philadelphia in the sixties. I called one of the wives we had known during the school years — the forties — to ask if she would be wearing a long dress for the gala banquet. She snarled at me.

"I won't be going to your blasted reunion. Maybe George will. He's living down the road from here with his new common-law wife. I don't give a hoot what you wear!"

That's when John started going to reunions of strangers.

Since I have been a widow I still avoid class reunions, but I did go with my sister to hers. That was interesting. The star of the weekend was a smart-looking blonde whom everyone agreed had been "Miss Dowdy of 1944" when last seen in the old home town. She had come all the way from Memphis on the advice of her analyst — to rid herself of girlhood frustrations and get even, I suppose. She set out to divest herself of every adolescent neurosis known to popular or medical science by ripping her astonished classmates up one side and down the other.

She must have had years of assertiveness training. Her life had been virtually *ruined* by that high school and the snooty Sub Deb Club. She had been angry about it for forty years, but she made up for the whole traumatic experience in two days. She left raving about having had a marvelous time.

Luckily, my husband never ran into her kind when he was gate-crashing. She would have ruined his whole evening.

When I hear old grads talking now about going to reunions, I'm sure someone, somewhere, is saying to his wife, "I wonder if that fat guy will be there?"

☙

## "SOUNDS SO MUCH LIKE 'UMBRELLA'"

My cousin Barbara says strange things, once in a while. I think her brain and her tongue become disconnected. Generally, that brings forth confusing conversation.

One day Barbara insisted, "Now when you get to Santa Barbara you must look up my husband's cousin. She's a lovely woman. You'll enjoy meeting her. She's lived out there for years. Her name is Trudy Pearsall. You can remember that easily because it sounds so much like 'umbrella.'"

Obviously Barbara's communicative parts had become unplugged again.

But I figured out what she meant.

Santa Barbara in June means Writers Conference for me. I had no time to call anyone's cousin, but I didn't tell Barbara.

About three years later, far from my Colorado home, a peculiar thing happened. With Lindblad Tours I was cruising the wondrous Swedish Archipelago. On an island in some place named the Bay of Bothnia, I sat on a bench at an outdoor museum to rest. I felt thoroughly immersed in Swedish culture when a woman seated herself on the bench beside me.

After the usual comments about Scandinavian wonders, we turned to personal conversation.

"Where is your home?" I said, predictably.

"Santa Barbara."

"Oh, I love Santa Barbara. I go there for a writers conference."

"How nice. And where is your home?"

"Colorado."

"How nice," she repeated. "I have a cousin who is a banker in Colorado."

"And your name is Trudy Pearsall," I replied quietly.

She stared.

"How could you possibly know my name?"

I said, of course, "Because it sounds so much like 'umbrella.'"

&

## COLLEGE PREP

I should have made a tape of the lecture I received on the eve of my departure for my second college career.

When my number one son offered me a cup of coffee, ushered me to the big armchair in the living room, and said, "Mother, we need to have a talk with you,"

I was uneasy.

Then the rest of them encircled me like Indians on the prairie preparing for an attack on the wagon — three sons, two daughters-in-law, and five solemn grandchildren. I shuddered.

"Tomorrow you will be heading east for college and we want you to realize . . ."

Heavens! It was the complete spiel — College Prep 101!

"Now, remember the real reason for going to school. You're not there just to have a good time with all of your friends."

I was admonished about making full use of the opportunities of college life: spend a lot of time in the library, take courses that will be a challenge.

"Don't take the easy stuff, Mom. You're not really a dummy, you know."

Of course, I was cautioned about getting too involved in extracurricular activities too soon. What was that supposed to mean? Wait until next fall to run for Homecoming Queen?

I was too stunned to speak. Then they started on the money. Surely I would need a carefully planned budget. Cafeteria food isn't all that bad.

Used textbooks were good enough for my purposes — especially since I was already laying out out-of-state tuition. Credit cards were only for emergencies.

Campus dress codes were explained. "Anything goes, nowadays. Not like when you were at Kansas State."

"For Pete's sake, Mom, don't buy a new wardrobe. You have plenty of old stuff that's good enough."

So it went — warnings about keeping up with my homework, lectures about five-year goals and being the best of whatever I might choose to be. They stopped just short of reminding me about pregnancy.

I asked why they didn't give Sarah a lecture. She was starting school, too — kindergarten. My feeble attempt at humor was not amusing to them, but Sarah climbed into my lap. That made us both feel better.

My daughters-in-law came to my rescue. "Just get off your mother's back. She's going to have a good time at Lake George."

Their husbands glared. I was delighted when it was finished. In all of the years of delivering these speeches to them, their father and I never knew whether they'd listened, let alone had memorized what we'd said. Now I was getting it back, verbatim.

After thanking them politely for their concern, I did remark about how proud their dad would have been to hear them quoting him so accurately. Then I headed off to upstate New York to do exactly as I wanted to — just as they had done when they went to college.

℘

# AUNT MILLIE'S GREAT GETAWAY

It didn't take much to upset Aunt Millie. We could get her going without much effort, probably because she had no children of her own. Looking back, I believe almost every family used to have an Aunt Millie. She looked after Granddad after Grandmother died. Aunt Millie and Uncle Ed lived with Granddad, as a matter of fact. Aunt Millie managed that very well. Only kids upset her.

Back in the '30s on Terracina Boulevard in Redlands, California, at least six of us pre-teen girls ordered — ordered! — Aunt Millie to stop the car. We wanted to pick magnolias off a tree beside the road. We could pin them in our hair when we went to the Redlands Bowl all dressed up.

Don't pin this one on me. I didn't have enough hair to pin anything in — or on, for that matter. But insist we did. Aunt Millie stopped.

The fact that she was driving Grandad's car complicated the escapade. Granddad gloried in his 1923 Cadillac even though it embarrassed us girls.

That car was not streamlined, and this was the '30s. Kids at school knew words like "Airflow" but we were riding in a big old green box on wheels. The horn went *oooogah*. It must have driven like a Mack truck. The upholstery scratched your legs. The oval windows made the back seat like a cave. Just stepping up on the running board to get into the old crate felt like climbing the Great Wall of China. Old ladies needed help. I'd give my right arm for that car now.

But there sat Aunt Millie at the wheel of the getaway car while we stole magnolias from the neighbor's tree by the road. Just as if she were stationed at the curb in front of Bank of America waiting for someone named Bugsy to leap into the back seat, tossing moneybags in front of him and shouting "Get goin', baby, I had to shoot the bastard!"

She revved that old motor so hard it probably could be heard three blocks away.

Some of the magnolias had brown spots. The best ones blossomed just out of reach. It took a while. To our diminutive aunt pounding on that pedal it seemed hours. She was so upset, in fact, that it never occurred to her that Grandad's house was just down the block. We could easily walk home.

When at last we piled back into the car Aunt Millie muttered something unfit for young ears and let out the clutch with the engine roaring. We took off like the man at the circus leaving the cannon, only backward. Our dear aunt had mixed up on the gears. We shot straight backward into Terracina Boulevard, whooping in the back seat while Aunt Millie stopped worrying about what words were fit for young ears. That old Cadillac screeched to a halt. The gears sounded more like a locomotive as she jammed that handle into place, tires squealed, and we made the turn to our driveway on two wooden wheels.

Last month, driving into Redlands, California, I needed a place to stay. Since Aunt Millie died, no family remains there. I headed down Terracina Boulevard hoping for a familiar sight — and there it stood: The magnolia tree!

Beside it? A sign reading, BED AND BREAKFAST, MOREY MANSION.
We both stayed that night.

കൗ

# ONE MORE ROOSTER FOR MOTHER

Christmas left a lot to be desired last year, especially about the gift for my mother. Mother will be ninety-two this year. It seemed to me I should find something special just to reward her for being gracious about so many other of my Christmas offerings. Some of the stuff I had made for her or decided she'd cherish through these last sixty years of my gifting fell short of the mark, I know.

These days I don't see Mother that much, but I did determine that I'd think of something to remind her every day that I'm thinking about her. After all, she doesn't get out much, any more.

What to buy — order from a catalogue? She certainly can't use any more sweaters or house slippers. Gadgets for her kitchen are useless. Works of art would crowd her walls. Jewelry would sit in her overloaded box. Seeds from fancy jams and preserves would gum up her teeth.

You have the same problems if your mother has reached this age. What do you do?

All of Mother's life she has had a collection of roosters. Over the years I've known her — sixty-seven — to be exact, anyone west of any given point has presented my mother with a rooster for her collection. How many she has accumulated I cannot say. How many she has dusted over the years would be anybody's guess. Some, the choice specimens, are displayed on shelves in her home. They vary from pewter cocks to straw roosters to porcelain to Lalique crystal, from two inches to twelve, roughly.

At her age, I reasoned, what Mother ought to have for Christmas would be a real chicken. Not a live chicken, mind you. Her carpet and her nerves couldn't take that. But a real chicken. That certainly would be different. The ultimate of chickenhood.

As luck would have it, last fall I was seated next to an old friend at a luncheon. She told me of the latest addition to her decor. You guessed it! Ruth, my friend, raved about two mounted roosters now gracing her dining room table. Almost a spooky coincidence, and I took full advantage. Ruth provided details.

In order to give your mother a stuffed chicken you need an understanding taxidermist. That had not occurred to me. One fine gentleman in Albuquerque willingly discussed the project with me, but he might not be able to meet the Christmas deadline. First, he had to find the right rooster. I told him to proceed, on faith, but by this time my enthusiasm had reached the I-must-have-this-chicken point. I'd need a backup, just in case.

On my local Pueblo scene I went into the whirling-dervish act through the yellow pages. Taxidermists one by one expressed astonishment over my request. Basic answer: "Look, lady, we mount pheasants, quail, deer, elk — bears, even — but not chickens." One guy just yelled, "Chickens!" at me. Finally, one kind woman named Jackie gave me the number I needed.

Those people specialized in putting fish on the wall, but they managed to get me a chicken. One white rooster standing on a rough log, proud as anything. I gave that to my daughter.

The Albuquerque rooster was lustrous, gleaming black. I gave that one to my mom.

&

# JUST FORGET THE RADIO AND DRIVE!

Miss Sarah has her learner's permit. Does this surprise you? For those of you who have been with this column — more or less — for the past eight years, the fact that my youngest granddaughter now qualifies as a beginning driver might come as a shock. Time has flown since Miss Sarah and I discovered the museum at Cañon City or started on our quest for the perfect cheeseburger, both events recorded on these pages.

I have contended for years that nothing puts a strain on family harmony to compare with the disruptions brought on by a learner's permit. Grown men cry. Teen tantrums reach a peak. Mothers cringe in the passenger seat in despair, just hoping to survive to see the old home place once more without knocking down the fence or destroying sprinklers beside the driveway.

Did we have learner's permits back in ancient days when you and I started to drive? We certainly had never heard of drivers' ed, I know that. Seems to me we were taken to some country road, straight and flat, and taught to drive. Shifting gears made the most trouble. That clutch business gave me fits. Of course, I became driver's age during The War, so gas rationing cut down on any teen driving at all.

As I recall, our father told my sisters and me we couldn't learn to drive until we learned to type. The logic in that attitude still escapes me, although typing would have come in handy for filling out the insurance claims. I still cannot type. My driving wins no prizes or commendations, either, but I do recall with something close to horror the days our children took the wheel.

Allison, oldest, broke John and me in on the ordeal for her younger brothers. She turned sixteen in June, so spring was her "training period." Allison has always coped, always tried. But in the spring in Colorado the air is filled with millers — those pesky flying dust-catchers that swarm everywhere. Nothing irritated Allison more than millers swarming in her vicinity. Our car had no air-conditioning in the sixties, so the windows had to be open while Allison practiced driving. She did just fine until a miller flew in. She forgot to hang on to the steering wheel. She tried to get out of the car without remembering to stop. Drivers unfortunate enough to be on the same street drove over curbs to get out of the way.

Now she's an excellent driver. With the windows closed.

Chris had his own Model A. He had practiced up and down the alley for two reasons: freedom from oncoming traffic and easy access to water. The radiator leaked profusely, so the garden hose was kept at the ready to keep the old Ford going.

When Chris did get out on the road, with his terrified mother riding shotgun, we could get as far as the home of our friends, the Belchers, five blocks from our house. There the Belcher boys waited with their garden hose to make sure we could get back to the safety of our own driveway.

Now Sarah wants to learn to drive and change stations on the radio at the same time. I'll just watch and listen, thanks.

⁂

## OMA MADE IT TO THE GARDEN

No matter how often I carry on about the joys of being at this stage of my life, I never fail to marvel at the fun to be had grandparenting. I honestly thought I'd reached the pinnacle of this "Oma" part of my life when I was privileged to accompany high-school-junior Jason on his rounds of the Eastern colleges hounding him about playing basketball. The experience was new to both of us. We toured West Point, Princeton, Columbia, Yale, and Harvard campuses one hot summer, listening to coaches and looking at dormitories and gyms.

Jason chose Stanford instead. Said he needed blue skies (and earthquakes?). However, the greatest thrill for that kid from Colorado has stuck in my mind:

The coaches at Columbia in New York City took this boy they hoped to recruit to see the most convincing sight they could muster in all of the city — Madison Square Garden.

That trip out to Columbia Jason did without Oma. No need for a grandmother to drag along when this sixteen-year-old swears he can get around in New York City on his own. I shuddered, since I've been known to be pretty well lost in Denver.

But off to Columbia he went, and we both lived through it.

Jason came back to our hotel walking — no, floating — four feet off the ground. He seemed as high as he goes when he jumps for a lay-up under the basket on the court — at least four feet. Princeton had been fine, West Point had been impressive, but now Jason had stood in Madison Square Garden. Had stood right there on the floor in Madison Square Garden! Harvard had little to offer that could compare. Yale flunked the Jason test entirely. The pilgrim had been to Mecca!

Now, what more could a grandmother expect of life than sharing such joy? Not much, I figured, until word reached upstate New York that Stanford would play in the NIT.

Being an old Big Eight follower, I knew NIT. Big time! National Invitational Tournament. Finals in — you know — Madison Square Garden. This grandma didn't miss a score or a game through the playoffs. If that kid went with his team to — heavens! I did wish they'd played on Eastern Time! Watching TV games at 2 a.m. can make the old girl glassy-eyed. But here came Stanford.

Certainly the calendar bulged with obligations of my own for speeches and such, but in New York, thank goodness. One or two adjustments of travel time and I could manage Madison Square Garden. Same hotel with the team. We made it, folks!

Stanford won the tournament, much to the amazement of the "experts" who touted Colorado and Oklahoma. Stanford won even though Jason did not play.

Granted, the day may come when, as an upperclassman, Jason will be leading the pack out there, making all the scores, playing for all the marbles. That day will probably come with such a fine school, such a great team and such a coach, but the thrill will never be greater than mine, seeing that kid, wearing Stanford colors, in the Garden.

I'll never ask for more than that.

❧

## NO WONDER THEY CALL THEM TURKEYS!

**W**ell, we had Thanksgiving dinner at my house. The turkey won again.

I cannot say how many years ago I last prepared dinner for the family for Thanksgiving. I haven't even been home for this holiday for quite a while. The joy of being in the bosom of the beloved family got the best of me. I said I'd do the turkey, the potatoes and some salad if the rest of them pitched in.

I should have stuck to the potatoes and the salad. In intervening years I had forgotten about my experience with turkeys. Might even be some sort of an unconscious blackout.

I picked out a fresh turkey at the market. Not the largest. When I did lug it into the house I discovered the tag read twenty pounds, which startled me but I tried fitting it into the roasting pan and shoving it into the oven. That worked.

Then I read the directions about time and temperature. Don't ever do that. You cannot trust those folks who label turkeys. They have some sort of a conspiracy going. I should have recalled all of those undercooked turkeys literally bleeding all over my best silver platters from other days. I should have turned up the heat, left the bird to its own devices at three o'clock in the morning, and gone back to bed.

After five hours at three twenty-five I had one beautifully browned twenty-pounder stuffed with the finest of cornbread, spices, giblets, celery, apples, raisins, and dried cherries to absolutely astonish my adoring tribe. Chris I chose to carve. After all, he's number one son.

There it was again — all that bloody juice on my best silver tray!

My sons "nuked" the legs of the turkey in the microwave. I tossed the salad and brought out the old-reliable Weaver potatoes (boiled potatoes, sour cream, jack cheese, and green chilies). We have had Weaver potatoes since the kids admitted they could not stand my gravy.

Thanks to the contributions of the rest of the crowd, we had more good food on hand than anyone will ever need. Perhaps they anticipated the problems I have with turkeys. After all, when they were growing up, their father always had more than enough stand-by food just in case I tried to serve raw turkey. That made Thanksgiving classic at our house.

You should have seen those Thanksgivings when the lord and master of Grand Avenue chose to expand our menu by roasting a pig in the back yard. Just in case the turkey . . .

John and the boys dug a pit, built a fire, put up this borrowed spit made of lead pipe, and skewered one small pig stuffed with apples and such. No better than roasting marshmallows at Girl Scout camp, our fire was either flaming all over the pig or too low to get it warm, even. Since John wanted to be sure this meat was thoroughly cooked, he roused the entire family to gather in the back yard to participate in such a family event. Before dawn the kids had each turned the handle to rotate the beast over the reluctant coals. By the time the sun came up the children and their father were back in bed, warm and toasty. The dogs and I watched the charred pig. Before breakfast, good old Dad had started the beef roast.

This Thanksgiving beat that one.

Christmas? We'll have ham.

&

## "WE TOOK TURNS"

After I'm dead and gone I hope somebody will find something to laugh about if my name ever comes up.

That sounds like a silly statement, doesn't it? At least it sounded silly to me until last week, after I had finished a presentation for a group of widowed persons.

I had told a couple of funny stories about my husband. I cannot say "my late husband" because John Weaver was never late anywhere in his life and calling him "late" would infuriate him. These anecdotes added, I thought, to my contention that we all have had some entertaining and amusing times of our lives that we mustn't forget after our lives have been changed "in the course of human events."

The story in question — questioned by a sad-faced lady from the audience — had to do with my method of getting even with John for inflicting his insomnia on me. I hid his removable false teeth ("bridges") in his shaving kit and left a quarter by the bathroom sink after he finally fell asleep about 5 a.m. After his fussing and fuming about the disappearance of his precious partial dentures, he spotted the quarter and accused me of being the world's cheapest tooth fairy. We both laughed a lot.

Matter of fact, he told me I'd have to stop laughing during breakfast at that hotel because people would think we weren't married. I like to tell that. Doesn't hurt anybody.

But this lady said she had never thought it "proper" to tell funny stories about people who have died. I say if that person added happiness and fun to your life the most fitting way to remember him or her is by recalling the good times. Seldom do I meet one of John's patients without hearing another "Let me tell you what Doc said . . ." It's always something to laugh about. After twelve years, I'd say that's a real compliment.

Never, I mean never, does the conversation among our family turn to any familiar subject without one of us repeating whatever Dad said or did, which brings laughter, which he would have enjoyed the most. Of course, there are other fitting memorials for those who have died, but for me and for John, I'm sure, a good laugh beats a bucketful of peonies any time.

Our family members have been real people. Trying to construct some sort of sainthood for my dad, my husband, or any of the rest would not be "suitable." We'll give credit where credit is due and enjoy to the utmost the good times we all shared.

Here's one more story I enjoy telling about John Weaver:

Years ago we were participating in some sort of a regional meeting for bank board members or some such at Bishops Lodge in New Mexico. Highlight of the stay was a breakfast ride. On the day before the early-morning trail trip to the breakfast camp we were all matched up with the horses at the ranch.

John Weaver weighed in at 250 pounds or more. The wrangler took one look and said, "You're ridin' Sherman, Doc."

Sherman suited his name. Built like a tank. At the end of the ride — no more than an hour — all of the crowd hooted and yelled at the fat doctor on the huge horse.

"How'd you and Sherman get along on the trail, Doc?"

John grinned. "Just fine. We took turns."

℘

# VIII. VESTA

Whenever I buy White Cloud bathroom tissue I think of Vesta. Other women might have more esthetic reminders of their mothers-in-law, but none more persistent than mine. There was a lot to know, criticize, and/or appreciate about Vesta Weaver, but the sight of a shelf filled with toilet paper distills for me the woman, her character and her life — especially the end of her life.

In July, 1965, Vesta and I went to the grocery store together for the last time. Joe went with us, for a change. Before leaving the house Vesta prepared a list written with obvious care and effort. As I drove down Republican Street to downtown Concordia, Kansas, on that hot day, Vesta was explaining the grocery list and the process of shopping to Joe as she would to a small child with a handful of dimes. When I parked the car in the lot next to Bogart's Market, I swallowed hard. This would not be easy. Joe Weaver was seventy years old. Until this summer he had never shopped for groceries — not in his whole life. That was Vesta's job.

"You're going to need to know how to do this, Joe," she said quietly as we got out of the car. "It can be fun. Relax."

Inside the store she pointed out the aisles of cereal, dog food, cleaning supplies and paper products. Joe walked ahead of us with the cart.

"This is the third time we've done this," she whispered to me. "Watch. He misses about half the list but he always buys toilet paper."

"Toilet paper?"

"That's it. Every time, he buys more toilet paper. We must have a six-month supply from the last two trips. There he goes again."

Vesta's cotton house dress hung from her once broad shoulders like a shroud. Her eyes shone in her bony face. Even her eyeglasses and false teeth seemed too big. She took my arm for support, then smiled.

Joe and I carried the sacks to the kitchen table. Vesta insisted that he put all the supplies away himself. "You'll need to know where things are." Knowing where anything was had always been Vesta's job.

Vesta and I talked a lot during that visit, just as we had through the twenty years we had been in-laws. She was the most pragmatic woman I shall ever know. She made a fetish of being down to earth — unspoiled. Having no affectations was almost an affectation of her own.

"Cheese is cheese," she'd remark when I would proudly present a gourmet recipe. "No sense in all those fancy foreign names. We'll use good old rat-trap cheese."

When the bed was unmade: "It felt good when you got out of it this morning, didn't it?"

She was Vesta to everyone in town, even her children and grandchildren. "None of that high-sounding Mrs. Weaver stuff for me or some cutesy name like Mumsie or Granny. Just call me Vesta. That's my name."

Grandkids loved to visit. Rides in the country with Joe and Vesta were childhood treats, especially when Vesta would whistle or hum. Her voice was a little like a calliope but a ride over to the old family farm was reason for rejoicing, so Vesta sang. When Joe's driving was too much "like Barney Oldfield," Vesta changed her tune to *Nearer My God to Thee*. The children squealed, and Joe slowed down.

About a spot on a skirt or a child's uncombed hair Vesta would say, "A man on a galloping horse would never see it." About cancer, when the surgeons simply closed her abdomen with no hope of recovery: "They say one person in four is going to die of cancer. I don't know why I wouldn't be one of them."

Facing reality, even terminal cancer, was not anything her husband was ready to do. That was Vesta's job, too — facing reality.

The arrangement they called marriage was a simple one: Joe worked at the post office; Vesta worked at everything else.

Growing up on a farm in Cloud County, Kansas, had not been a childhood filled with wonder and delight. Motherless at seven or eight, Vesta cared for her brother and sister and took orders from her father. After two years of college ("enough for any girl"), she married and took orders from Joe. To her that was the way life goes.

Never in her life did she wear high heels or slacks or a diamond ring. Never did she play bridge or go to lunch with the girls. Never did she go the forty miles to Salina to shop. She never had a car or a bank account of her own. Neither — in her own mind — did she lack the absolute necessities of life. I never heard her whine. Never saw her complain.

In the summer of her forty-eighth year of marriage she said, "I guess I should have seen to it Joe could take care of himself. It's hard for him to learn now." My insides churned and my face must have been crimson, recalling the hundreds — thousands — of times I had sworn under my breath at that chauvinistic sonovabitch demanding to be waited on with the same smug "that's Vesta's job."

In those last months she showed him how to wash his clothes, do his dishes, iron shirts, pay utility bills, find socks, get the car serviced, mow the lawn, and call the plumber. She taught him about frozen foods, how to operate the can opener. She demonstrated changing sheets when she could scarcely stand.

Then in August of 1965, satisfied that she had done the best she could to prepare her husband for life without her, she took to her bed and died as matter-of-factly as she had lived.

"Don't take me back to the hospital," she commanded, "I'll have to be here to make sure Joe gets along all right."

She helped him find her good black dress, arranged for her sister to braid her hair. So the priest came and she said her prayers and that was that.

Vesta Weaver had never considered herself "special." I don't think she had any idea of how much she was respected for her let's-just-get-on-with-it attitude. She would have been astonished by her own funeral. The church and the parish hall were filled to overflowing with her friends and admirers. The Bishop came from Topeka. Senator Carlson came from Washington.

Vesta had made her point: That's the way life is.

She was quite a woman. I never really understood the way she lived, but I certainly learned a lot from the way she died.

◦↔

THERE'S MORE TO ME THAN I'VE USED YET

# "Age is a matter of mind. When our minds are kept active we become more interesting through our personal growth."

— M. P., Norwood, Massachusetts

How one reader reacted to Frances Weaver's

## *The Girls with the Grandmother Faces*

She finally smiled and we walked on to Worcester College for another class.

Believe me, I don't go around with my soapbox delivering this tirade to every woman I meet — just the ones I think can take it. There are a lot of them.

More than half of the women over sixty-five in America are widows. Older women are also the fastest-growing segment of our population. In terms of absolute numbers, that means there are literally millions of women who no longer have husbands.

So why do so many of the widows I meet act as if this "catastrophe" had never happened to anyone but themselves? Why do some of the brighter ladies have such a tough time accepting their new role in life? That's for the psychologists to answer, certainly, but my own deduction is that loss of married life takes away a safety net. We have used our husbands and our families as a shield, a buffer, an excuse for not making our own decisions or recognizing our own capabilities. Younger women have gotten into this "self-fullfillment" business. We who are in our sixties have not made that commitment to ourselves until we are suddenly on our own. We have to play catch-up.

For years I have been acquainted with a woman

To order, write or call
Midlife Musings, Publisher
P. O. Box 970
Saratoga Springs
New York 12866
(800) 842-7229

MIDLIFE MUSINGS

Saratoga Springs
New York

ISBN 0-9617930-2-3  $7.95 U.S., $9.95 CANADA

# "I am a grandmother, but not a widow. I realized there was a message for all of us!"

— M. H., Green Bay, Wisconsin

A readers's analysis of
Frances Weaver's

## *Where Do Grandmothers Come From? (And Where Do They Go?)*

To order, write or call
Midlife Musings, Publisher
P. O. Box 970
Saratoga Springs
New York 12866
(800) 842-7229

**MIDLIFE MUSINGS**

Saratoga Springs
New York

basically pleasant, warm and safe. It took me six months to recover from a ruptured appendix, but recover I did.

In looking back over those long-gone days when chicken pox meant a sign on your house and polio ran rampant, it's the details that fill in the picture. Our lives, of my family and me, fit the pattern of mid-American middle-class morality. Who couldn't grow up "happy" under such circumstances? We lived in such a stable community we actually studied under some of the same teachers who had taught our parents. Everyone in town was our friend.

Meanwhile, we girls had the expected gripes:

Mother wouldn't let us wear lipstick.

Mother wouldn't allow us to hang around Hubbell's much.

Mother made us wear winter underwear 'til Easter.

Mother didn't let us drive as soon as our friends did.

Mother wouldn't let us call up the boys.

Mother always knew when we tried to smoke.

Mother never really trusted any of us, including Dad.

She still doesn't.

ISBN 0-9617930-4-X  $10 U. S., $12 CANADA

# "We just didn't want that book to end!"

— F. R., Neotsu, Oregon

One of the many compliments for Frances Weaver's novel

## *Golden Roamers*

ever seen him, put his arms around this girl, looked straight up at heaven, and guided her to the bus.

"Home to the Bengstons," he said.

Those Bengstons turned out to be really nice people. The sight of our coach coming up their lane had to startle them a bit, and they were more than grateful about our giving Julie and her precious children the ride over to the farm. All in all, Emmett Coleman had handled the entire situation in stride, even Lanning's rude criticism of the poor distraught girl.

I hate to sound like an out-and-out Calvinist, but it did seem Fate had taken a hand in this affair. Ruth hugged her old neighbors with a joy I had never seen in her. Bess glowed in Ruth's happiness, really. It didn't take long for word to spread about the Colemans and their help for Julie. And their garish bus.

In the midst of all this commotion, I looked around for Emmett. Where was he? Pouting behind the barn? Hunkering alone in the old outhouse? Oh, no! I found Emmett leaning casually against the tailgate of a pickup. He was telling a dozen awe-struck Iowa farmers about carrots as big as your arm, and "tomatoes ripe all year 'round."

"'Course we have dates on the tree — and all

To order, write or call
Midlife Musings, Publisher
P. O. Box 970
Saratoga Springs
New York 12866
(800) 842-7229

**MIDLIFE MUSINGS**

Saratoga Springs
New York

ISBN 0-9617930-5-8  $10 U.S., $12 CANADA